CIRCULAR TIME

Visiting Scotland's Stone Circles & Cairns

Loren Cruden

To my mother's lineage of MacKinnons; and to Rob, who welcomed their descendent back to Skye. Cheers!

Table of Contents

Acknowledgements vi

Introduction 1

Stone Circles and Cairns in Historical Context.............10

Distribution of Scottish Stone Circles and Henge Monuments..11

Cairns, Circles, & Henges 12

Distribution of Selected Sites 18

Isle of Arran 19

    Stronach Wood 21

    Lamlash..22

    Machrie Moor 22

    Additional Sites...29

Argyll 34

    Achnabreck 36

    Cairnbaan 39

    Dunadd 41

    Kilmartin Monuments...42

    Ford Digression..57

    Kintraw 61

    Strontoiller 64

Additional Sites 66
Isle of Mull 68
   Loch Buie 70
   Additional Sites 73
   The Road to Skye 74
Isle of Skye 79
   Na Clachan Bhreige 81
   Cnocan nan Gobhar 84
   Clach na h-Annait 85
   High Pasture Cave 86
   An Sithean & Cill Chriosd 86
   Liveras 87
   Additional Sites 88
Western Isles 90
   Isle of Lewis 91
      Calanais 91
      Calanais Satellite Circles 97
   North Uist 99
      Caranais 99
      Barpa Longais 100
      Pobull Fhinn 100
      Marrogh 101
      Loch a'Phobuill 102
      Unival 102

iii

Additional Sites 103
Inverness-shire 105
   Corrimony 106
   Balnuaran of Clava 107
   Additional Sites; also Sutherland Sites 112
Caithness 120
   Guidebest 122
   Achavanich 123
   The Grey Cairns of Camster 124
   Hill o'Many Stones/Mid-Cyth Stone Rows 127
   Garrywhin/Cairn of Get 128
   Additional Sites 129
Orkney 132
   Stones of Stenness 134
   Ring of Brogar/Brodgar 136
   Maes Howe 139
   Additional Sites; also Shetland Sites 141
Aberdeenshire 151
   Moray & Banffshire Sites 157
   Loanhead of Daviot 160
   Old Keig 162
   Cullerie 165
   Easter Aquorthies 165
   Tomnaverie 167
   Additional Sites 170

Kincardineshire & Angus Sites 185
Perthshire 191
Lundin Farm 192
Fortingall 194
Croft Morag 195
Additional Sites 198
Sites in Other Scottish Regions 206
Stone of Destiny 220
Appendices 228
Glossary 228
Regional Monument Styles 232
Circle Shapes & Astronomical Alignments 234
Resources 237
Bibliography 240
Site Index 247
About the Author 260

v

ACKNOWLEDGEMENTS

Thanks to my son, Gabriel Cruden, for his vital help with the companion map to this guidebook; and to Kenny Steven for permission to use his poem.

Thanks to Rob Kerr for navigating us around the country, for substantial input on the manuscript – including the circle-shape and alignment explanations for the appendix – and for his insights and companionship.

Thanks to archivists and librarians on Skye who generously gave access to survey reports; to Martin Wildgoose for the Camas Daraich walk; and to all who mapped the way before us.

In the U.S., thanks to Alanna Hudis for the care with which she transcribes my manuscripts to disks; to Martha, for her painstakingly turning the manuscript into a book; and to Gabriel, for help in all things.

To see the past in its place
different from the present
yet with the presence of the present,
for history is a pattern of timeless moment.

T.S. Eliot

Introduction

The Mesolithic inhabitants of Scotland were hunter-gatherers who left little trace of their tenure. Like their contemporaries in other parts of the world, they lived intimately with their environment, developing a wisdom of relationship to place, and among neighbouring groups, enabling small, mobile communities to survive and prosper. During Neolithic times, as agriculture became a focus, this process became more settled and elaborate. For the megalith ("big stone") builders, their monument technology probably peaked with the creation of Stonehenge, an accomplishment that still awes us thousands of years after its completion.

Early societies in Scotland, through to the Iron Age Celts, were oral cultures. Knowledge was transmitted verbally. In Neolithic society short life expectancies would make transmission of knowledge all the more urgent, and regard for elders and ancestors all the more likely. But if individual life was brief, close at hand was a medium far more enduring: stone.

People in Scotland throughout the ages seem to have had a particular feel for stone. So much of Scotland IS stone – visible, compelling, definitive – and much of it very old.

There are hundreds of Neolithic and Bronze Age stone circles and cairns in Scotland. Many are situated and configured to facilitate astronomical observations. Many clearly are also associated with burial or cremation practices. Speculation abounds on the intentions behind, and ceremonial uses of, the ancient circles. The effect of planting megaliths upright in the ground is striking – literally turning time on end. Layers of geological time held in stone, turned vertical between earth and sky, delineating portals and avenues through which light – life - moves in regenerative cycles.

E.C. Krupp says "…ideas about the structures of the world, about the rhythms of time and about the origin of the cosmos are all combined into a ceremonial landscape." And, "Influence over time, one way or another, is usually what we have in mind when we're talking power. We link power with the cause that produces effect."

Megalith builders were pattern specialists. Stellar patterns, moon and sun cycles, navigational alignments, territorial markers, engagement with natural fields and flows, seasonal patterns, death and renewal: it is possible all these were at least aspects of what stone circles were about. The circles were part of a choreography of human life within local and cosmic patterns, and the relationship of people to place; a concentric consciousness.

As Scotland's inhabitants traversed the Bronze Age, Neolithic monuments fell out of use. Hunter-gatherer society had long since been absorbed by a more settled agricultural lifestyle. Authority had become more centralized. Monuments proliferated during this era of nucleated settlement, before focus shifted to more portable and individual symbols of power – the metalworking of the Bronze Age.

Academics once assumed that prehistoric social changes were due to aggression or invasion. It is now realized that life in those days was far less brutish than supposed. According to Lewis Mumford, "Long before Bronze Age techniques had fully utilised the earlier improvements in horticulture and agriculture, archaic man had done the preliminary work of exploration so well that except for a few plants like the cultivated strawberry and the boysenberry, all our present domesticated plants and animals are Neolithic end-products."

What catalysed changes in prehistoric ways of life probably had more to do with environmental pressures and cultural borrowings and assimilations than with intertribal hostilities. Off the beaten track as Scotland is overland, from coastal European and North Atlantic regions it has always been readily accessible by boat. Traces of settlement on Scottish islands go back at least 8-10,000 years. With the retreat of the glaciers, climate in Scotland became favourable to humans; more favourable at times than it is today, certainly less wet.

Skimming prehistory, we see the styles of dwellings reflecting shifts in society: from seasonal encampments to stone and timber settlements, monumental architecture (increased centralization and territoriality), and, with the Bronze Age, abandonment of monumental architecture and an increase in portable prestige goods and material culture.

Popular misconception couples Neolithic stone circles with Celtic druids, but these structures were built long before the Iron Age – though may have been of interest to the druids. From Michael Newton: "The continuity of the styles of the buildings, the uninterrupted occupation of particular sites and the continued reverence of sacred sites...attests to a remarkable degree of cultural stability from early in the first millennium BCE well into the historic Celtic period..."

Embedded in this stability was a continued close observation of natural rhythms: tides, seasons, migrations, growth cycles, creative and destructive processes. Vulnerable human life needed

to move in step with the larger dance. Neolithic monuments suggest a painstaking attention to that movement. Chambered cairns, especially those passage-
graves designed to admit the winter solstice light on an inner chamber, point to committed participation in cycles of renewal.

Scottish folk tales refer to standing stones, healing stones, and so on, acknowledging a continuing regard for the ancient monuments. Whether we focus on Neolithic circles, Pictish symbol-stones, Celtic inaugural stone footprints, or even modern commemorative cairns and standing stones, we find a virtually unbroken tradition of cultural – and I dare say spiritual – representation in stone.

Na tursachan may be translated from Gaelic as "places of pilgrimage." Neolithic circles may've been places in which people gathered for ceremony or event, or to individually seek knowledge on behalf of community. Today these places still draw people from far and wide. Whatever the nature of that interest, beyond getting background about the sites themselves, I urge the visitor to acquire some knowledge of Scotland itself, its history and contemporary life. Knowledge not only enriches experience and puts what is experienced into context, but also helps guide the stranger into more mutually satisfying interactions. Scotland's stones and Scotland's people belong to one another.

In organizing this book, I selected a representative tour of sites. Eight regions are particularly featured: Orkney, Caithness, Inverness-shire, Aberdeen-shire, Argyll and her islands, the Isle of Skye, the Western Isles, and Perthshire. Some sites are described at length, others in compact fact sheets. Additional regions and sites are listed. The tour takes the traveller on a loop journey not only to some of the finest monuments, but also some of the finest landscapes in Scotland.

Comparisons among sites are as interesting as the sites themselves. When visiting many circles, especially within one region or during a compressed trip, a connectedness among sites may be discerned. Even over long distances, some sites seem to echo each other. Calanais on Lewis and the Brogar-Stenness complex on Orkney, for instance, are reminiscent of each other despite differing compositions.

Some of the things my companion and I discussed while travelling site to site included what might have been behind Neolithic builders' choice of specific shapes, sizes, arrangements, and rock types for their circles; why monuments are plentiful in some areas and not others; and how (and why) small populations could devote so much time and effort to massive monument building. The earliest monuments, in fact, required the most complex engineering and craftsmanship, but were obviously a priority of people not long removed from a hunter-gatherer lifestyle. What prompted them? Where did such knowledge and skill originate?

The monuments also provoke thought about contemporary use and attitudes – about whether or how best these sites should now be preserved and presented, and about what has been lost and what can be learned from traditional peoples' relationship with the cosmos – the stars, the land, and each other.

Standing stones are part of Scotland's historical landscape and consciousness, and now also part of its tourist industry. But the majority of sites still abide in the rural context of pastures and moors, or beside country roads where a traveller may be tempted to pause a while to muse among the stones.

Stone Circles and Cairns

in Historical Context

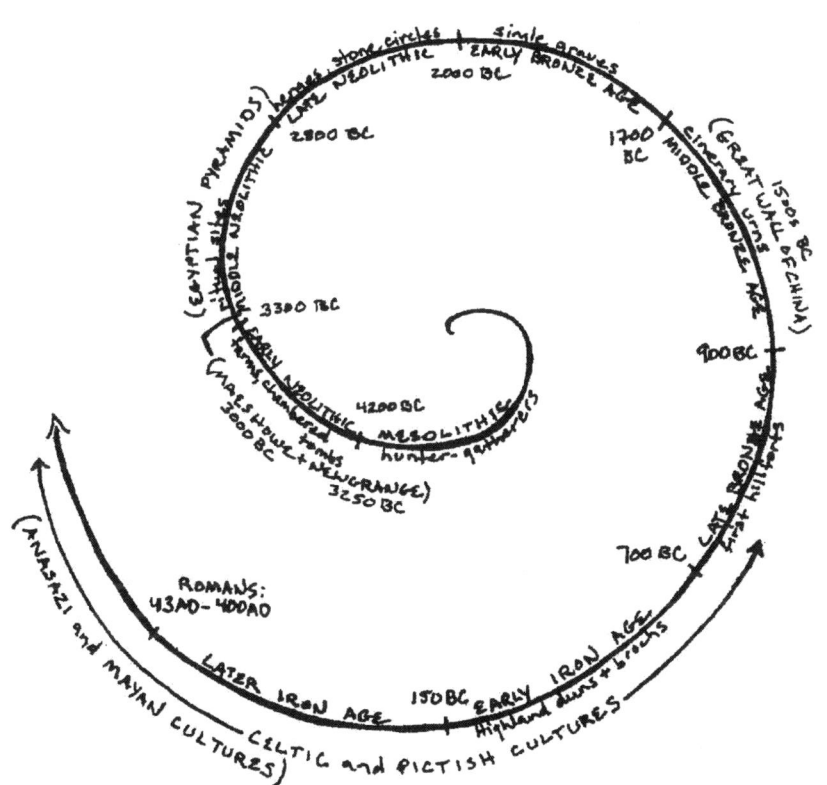

Distribution of Scottish Stone Circles and Henge Monuments

Cairns, Circles, & Henges

There are two basic tomb styles in Neolithic Scottish burial cairns: passage-graves/chambered cairns (a central chamber accessed by a passage) and gallery graves (often long cairns with chambers directly accessed from outside). Ring cairns are those with no passage or roof; the central area is open.

Chambered cairns were used for multiple or successive burials. Excarnation – bodies "pre-buried" or exposed, then later interred – was often practiced, as was cremation or partial cremation before interment. Communal passage-graves were the Neolithic norm in northern Scotland and Ireland. Scottish cairn types are further subdivided under the headings of: Clyde cairns, Hebridean cairns, Orkney-Cromarty cairns, and the Maes Howe group.

Life expectancy in those times was much shorter than today, but there is little evidence of warfare, invasion or violent conflict among individuals, and Neolithic dwellings were not built on defensive lines. In general people were a little smaller than today, but muscular – no evidence of a leisure class – and communal burials included people of all ages and both sexes. At least half the remains show signs of degenerative spinal deformities – a consequence of heavy labour; women's skulls often had cranial indentations from "browband" loads.

During the late Neolithic and early Bronze Age people began placing food, drink, tools, weapons, and personal goods with bodies. Burying beakers with the bodies became fashionable after 2000 BCE. Some five hundred chambered cairns survive in Scotland, spanning the period 4000 to 2000 BCE. Between 3000 and 2500 BCE the use of chambered tombs decreased and individual burials or cremations in simple mounds or cists increased. This decreased focus on monument tomb building coincided with an increase in building stone circles – perhaps a vertical shift of emphasis from earth to sky, or an increased linkage between earth and sky.

This is typical of centralized power, where settled communities produce social stratification, and leaders establish an anchored connection between themselves and cosmic structure and order. The agrarian and the hunter-gatherer relationships to environment and spiritual power differ profoundly from one another.

"Henges" are ritual areas delineated by ditches or banks, each henge having one or more causeways across the ditch/bank. Henges are unique to the United Kingdom. They sometimes, but not always, contain stone or timber circles. Stonehenge is the only henge circle featuring "hanging" or lintel stones in its construction. All the UK's circles and henges were built during the same prehistoric period. Many circles were made of timber instead of stone; little trace of these timber works remains, though some were very complex.

Henges tend to occur more in south and east parts of the UK, favouring low ground and stream or riverside locations, whereas stone circles occur more in Scotland, Wales, and Britain's west and north. Another configuration – stone rows – was constructed in Caithness and Sutherland. These take the form of single, double, or triple lines of many small stones, usually running from a large terminal stone or stones, up to a burial cairn.

Richard Bradley notes of Neolithic builders: "The character of the place seemed at least as important as the qualities of the material that were found there...people chose to quarry the stone in precisely those areas that were located furthest from the lower ground. The distinction between monuments and natural places may have been that between two ways of remembering the past and two ways of thinking about time."

Neolithic circles seem to mirror an environment, a recreated landscape incorporating past, present, and future. To suggest utilitarian use of stone circles, as observatories, navigational aids, or territorial markers, is not to imply they were any the less sacred as sites. Michael Newton notes that "The native intellectual traditions of primal societies can be highly expressive and sophisticated, without requiring the technical jargon characteristic of modernist science...This mythopoetic understanding of the cosmos allowing all topics of discourse to be discussed using the same language, rather than creating terminology which artificially segregates human civilisation and knowledge from the rest of nature." Thus, the physical and spiritual functions of Neolithic monuments probably have mutual implications.

Thinking about what has been discovered about the monuments, a picture of a multiplicity of communal activity encompassed in their precincts emerges. In selecting a perspective from which to appreciate these monuments, the visitor is spoiled for choice. A magnificent story, told in stone.

This guidebook is arranged as a loop tour beginning west of the Central Belt, going north along the west coast and Hebrides to the north-eastern mainland and up to Orkney; then down to the east and to Highland Perthshire, ending just above the Central Belt. Ordinance map coordinates are noted for each site listing.

The traveller can follow this loop as presented, do it in reverse, or access it however desired – visiting some sites/regions and not others; whatever suits. The listings of additional sites and regions may spark interest in tangents of the traveller's own devising.

The companion to this guidebook is "The Ancient Monuments Map of Scotland," published by Neil Wilson Publishing Ltd., Suite Ex 8, The Pentagon Centre, 44 Washington Street, Glasgow, G3 8AZ, Scotland.

Distribution of Selected Sites
(Shetland not shown)

The Isle of Arran

Arran is the largest and has the highest ground of any of the Firth of Clyde islands. Its high ground is a beautiful range of granite mountains on the island's northeast side, making Arran a magnet for hillwalkers and climbers as well as archaeology buffs.

The most usual way to reach Arran, especially from Glasgow, is by the ferry from Ardrossan to Brodick. On Arran, the A841 follows the coastline around the island, and the B880 cuts east-west across the middle of the island. If you do not have your own transport, there are bus services (limited in winter) and a PostBus on the north and south circular routes.

Brodick is the island's capital, and contains the main tourist office and other services. There are hotels, B&Bs, and self-catering accommodations around the island – Arran is a popular destination for Scots as well as visitors from abroad – and there are several hostels also. Blackwaterfoot, on the west coast, is the closest village to the main concentration of Neolithic sites. Blackwaterfoot can be reached directly from Brodick by going across the island on the B880, or by driving the loop road – an engaging scenic route.[1]

Arran's weather is changeable and often wet, like most of Scotland's west coast, but enjoyment is not hindered for the suitably outfitted.

Archaeology records reveal that people were living on Arran by 10,000 years ago. Farming began during the Neolithic period, along with the construction of communal tombs, which were in use for about a thousand years. The south part of Arran is studded with these chambered tombs, the largest human-made structures in the world at the time of their construction. Bronze Age tombs – small

---

[1] *Single-tracks* are the narrow paved roads found on many of the islands and some mainland areas. There are periodic bulges for allowing oncoming or faster following traffic to pass. Courtesy is the imperative in either case! Alertly pull over TO YOUR LEFT, and give a wave. Keep in mind that vehicles behind you may not want to crawl at a sightseer's uncertain pace; let them by. It is not only courteous, it is the law. Single-track driving is an artfully cooperative, not competitive, endeavour.

individual cists – are also in abundance on Arran, some of them incorporated into the older, larger Neolithic tombs.

Arriving in Brodick, pause to admire the **Stronach Standing Stone**, (NS 010 366), a red sandstone Bronze Age marker. From there a short detour just north and west of Brodick on the A880 leads to a rock art site, **Stronach Wood Cup & Ring Carvings**, (NS 003 363). When we visited this site there was no signage to guide us; my unfailing navigator directed us to a rutted dirt track where we parked, proceeding on foot up, up, and up between dense conifers to where the track ended at a decorated glacial slab.

Even when expected, the carvings are startling. We saw multiple cup & ring markings carved during the Bronze Age; numerous "keyhole" patterns lined with green moss, amid the morning's winter chill and the dark of the tree plantation. A perky robin kept us company as we gazed at the carvings, so old and silent, their meaning hidden under millennia.

Also off the B880, outside of Brodick, is the ***Deer Park*** site of standing stones, (NS 005 374).

Going south from Brodick, the next site is a stone circle halfway between Lamlash and Brodick, (NS 018 336). Only four granite boulders remain of this modest 22' configuration within which a cist was excavated. An outlier stone stands near, to the south. ***Lamlash Circle*** seems maybe a little forlorn beside the main road and forestry operations. The circle is unsignposted, perhaps unappreciated on an island that boasts wonders like Machrie Moor.

Machrie Moor

Off the A841, 2.25 miles NNE of Blackwaterfoot. (NR 912 324)

There is a tiny parking area opposite the signposted trail to Machrie Moor. The trail is a mile and a half walk to one of Europe's foremost ancient sites.

The stone circles of Machrie Moor – this name derived from the Gaelic *machair*, meaning a coastal stretch of level sandy ground – are thought to have been raised between 1800 and 1600 BCE. The moor is host to myriad dwellings and monuments dating from that period.

The first site encountered along the track that crosses sheep fields and moorland, is **Circle 10**, also known as the **Moss Farm Road Circle**, (though a hut site is located in the grazing to the right about halfway between the paved road and Circle #10). Due to damage from farm activity, this site looks more like a cairn than a stone circle, but circle it apparently once was, with a burial cist inside.

The burial cairn was enclosed by a true circle 71' in diameter, the stones of which are chiefly sandstone, while the cairn appears to have been built of substantial granite blocks. The inner chamber collapsed over time. This may be one of the older monuments on Machrie Moor, estimated to have been constructed circa 2000 BCE. Two standing stones on the southern perimeter of the monument seem to attribute some importance to that direction. This circle's stones are an interesting collection, especially the curvy sandstone that gives the circle a stylish look. Another feature that catches the eye is the way pairs of boulders at several places seem to nicely frame prominent hills north and east of Machrie.

There are at least 40 known Bronze Age and Neolithic stone circles, hut circles, chambered cairns, and standing stones in the Machrie Moor area alone, similar to Kilmartin, Calanais, and Orkney in its astonishing concentration of monuments. Arran teems with sites. There must have been good reason for this, as neighbouring islands do not have this plethora of ancient sites.

Continuing along the farm track, which winds toward the east, climbing a short rise, there are two solitary outliers, one on each side of the path at a distance of 100 yards or so. The one to the north has a modern companion, a commemorative engraved stone, recently placed. From this viewpoint the bustling Machrie Moor site can be seen in its entirety, a breathtaking array of stone circles.

Just above the ruins of Moss Farm – after passing a burial cist at the side of the track – is a splendid double circle of granite erratics. This circle is known as **Circle #5, Suidhe Choire Fhionn**, (the Seat of Fingal's Cauldron). It was built 4,000 years ago. The inner circle has eight stones and is an almost true circle. The outer ring, egg-shaped, has fifteen stones and a diameter of 59'. The most prominent stones are situated in the NE, ESE, and WSW. The symmetry suggests possible astronomical alignment. A stone in the outer circle is pierced by a hole, reputed to be the tethering post for Fingal's hound Bran. The remnants of a burial cist were found in the centre of this circle.

Circle #4, like Circle #5, is positioned to overlook the site complex. Circle #4 now consists of just four granite stones. If a circle, it is estimated to have been about 9.1 metres in diameter, but it could've been a 4-poster or even a 5-stone circle of the Irish style instead. During excavation in 1861, a central cist was discovered, containing fragments of bone along with flint arrowheads, a bronze bradawl, and a food vessel.

    Looking down slope from these circles, the gaze is arrested by what appears to be a huge outlier. But this 4.3 metre stone in part of a circle (*Circle #3*) whose other five stones are now broken stubs. Three additional circle stones are buried under the peat that has built up over the millennia. These stones may've been brought from the sea cliffs about two miles to the west. The size and relative fragility of these giant slabs must have made their transportation a backbreaking endeavour.

    When the circle was built it would have been egg-shaped – a diameter of 53'7" on the SSW-NNE axis, and 5.'5" on the perpendicular axis. Two cists were found within the circle – one central and one south of centre. They both contained flints, but the southern cist also contained skeletal parts of – as Burl reports – "a round-headed twenty-two-year old man."

On the late afternoon of our visit, the ruddy sandstone pillar, standing like a sentinel of the glen beyond, glowed warmly in the oblique winter light of the setting sun. The clouds above were a splash of magenta and tawny orange, the moor grasses tawny also, the hills luminous. An unforgettable scene; the monolith anchored in the eerie beauty of this lighted, wind-raked moor.

Circle #2 is the jewel in Machrie's crown, even with only 3 of its sandstone giants intact. Along with these three, five broken stones complete the circle's outline. The monoliths instantly call to mind the Stenness Stones in Orkney. They have the same pared shapes and abstract quality – austere, absolute – soaring upward, dwarfing the observer. They nail the attention. The triad stand on the west to northeast arc of a circle that was once 42' in diameter. The tallest of the three pillars is 14'5". On the opposite arc are two granite stones that have been engineered into millstones, but left in-situ. Two cists were found within this circle, both close to the centre. One contained flints and a food vessel, the other was empty.

Along with adjacent circles 1 and 11, this 4,000-year old arrangement was probably predated by a timber circle 5,000 years ago, but even earlier settlers left evidence of their sojourn in the form of pottery fragments dating from circa 3900 BCE.

Circle #1 is egg-shaped, aligned on the cross-quarter, and is constructed of 11 (once 12) stones arranged in a ring of alternating sandstone slabs and granite boulders.

Circle #11 was not excavated from the rising tide of peat until 1978. Like Circle #1, the stones apparently replaced an earlier timber structure. The present incarnation is a rough ring that does not correspond to any of the usual structure types. Of the 10 stones, 9 are sandstone with the north-eastern stone of granite. Several microliths, fragments of flint, scrapers, and knives were found in the interior, but nothing offering a date for the construction.

The circles of Machrie Moor all seem to share a similar orientation towards the northeast where Machrie Glen cuts eastward across the island. Standing within each of the circles and using the deep cut of Machrie Glen as a foresight, four of the rings are sited to indicate sunrise on midsummer morning, the other two circles are apparently "only slightly misplaced." These two (Circle #3 and #5), seem to have lunar orientations.

Additional Sites on Arran

Aucheleffan Stone Circle

- 5½ miles ESE of Blackwaterfoot. (NR 978 251) Drive north 1 mile from Torryline to the edge of the forest, then walk 2½ miles on an uphill track. Only for the hardy: difficult access.

- *Configuration*: Classic 4-Poster, the four stones making 16' square. The stones range from 2½ to almost 4' in height.

- *Alignment*: The 4 stones are exactly N-S and E-W of each other.

They once overlooked Ailsa Craig across the sea; now are surrounded by a forestry plantation.
- *Type of Stone*: Local granite.
- *Condition*: Good.

Auchengallon Cairn
- Off the A841, 4 miles north of Blackwaterfoot, on Machrie Bay, just east of the road. (NR 893 346) Very easy access.
- *Date*: Bronze Age, 3-4,000 years old.
- *Configuration*: A cairn surrounded by an irregular 15-stone, 47' circle that may have formed a kerb of a ruined cairn. The stones are height-gradated 3'-7'8", the tallest toward the sea, and some are missing, leaving a gap in the NE. The circle may be a "recumbent" variant.
- *Alignment*: On a ridge facing the sea.
- *Artifacts*: A stone cist was discovered within the cairn.

- *Type of Stone*: One stone on each side of the circle is grey granite, the rest are red sandstone.
- *Condition*: Recognizable.

Machrie Burn Stone Circle

- 6¼ miles west of Blackwaterfoot, 4½ miles north of Blackwaterfoot.
- A fair 1-mile ENE walk across the moor from Auchengallon. (NR 908 351)
- *Configuration*: Low stones forming a 4-Poster. There are also hut circles in the area.
- *Alignment*: NNE-SSW rectangle.
- *Type of Stone*: Granite
- *Condition*: Good

Other Additional Sites

Near Machrie Moor:

- *Druid Stone* (NR 886 293) Single Bronze Age stone.
- *Kilpatrick Cashel* (NR 906 261) Bronze Age cists in a Neolithic site.

Near the South Coast:
- *Carn Ban* (NR 991 262) Neolithic Clyde tomb.
- *Clachaig Chambered Tomb* (NR 949 212) Neolithic chambered tomb and Bronze Age cist.
- *East Bennon Chambered Tomb* (NR 994 207) Neolithic chambered tomb.
- *Torlin Chambered Tomb* (NR 955 211) Neolithic chambered tomb.

Near Whiting Bay:
- *Giant's Grave* (NS 044 246) Two Neolithic chambered tombs.

Near Sannox:
- *North Sannox Bronze Age Cairn* (NS 014 466) Bronze Age cist, standing stone.
- *Sannox Chambered Tomb* (NS 017 448) Neolithic tomb.
- *Sannox Standing Stones* (NS 015 458) Bronze Age

From Arran, we next move to the Argyll mainland to visit the Kilmartin monuments. The most direct route is to depart Arran's north coast on the Lochranza ferry to Tarbert, and from there drive or take a bus north on the A83 to Lochgilphead, picking up the A816 to Kilmartin. Alternately, in summer only, you can take the Lochranza ferry to Claonaig, in Kintyre, drive the B8001 to Kennacraig and pick up the A83 north from there.

Argyll

Living on the Isle of Skye, it is hard to be impressed by landscape elsewhere, but Argyll is exceptional, like something out of a fairytale, where you might wake one morning to find the landscape rearranged, or all the people vanished. In the words of Ronald W.B. Morris, "In Argyll and its isles the pagan gods are not so long dead."

Infusing this realm of mountain and glen, waterfall and burn, lochs deeply dividing luminous green land, is the rich indelible history of Dal Riata, the Kingdom of the Gaels. An Argyll trip, even more than most in Scotland, is a journey through layers of history. But for all the sturdy duration of human occupation, much of the countryside still seems to belong to itself. Mid-Argyll is studded with cairns; it also contains some of Scotland's premier rock art sites.

Cup-and-ring (C&R) markings are found all over the world; in appearance they are little scoops in the rock, surrounded by a circular groove. In the

UK, the main regions for finding rock art are between Inverness and Yorkshire.

Considering the large number of C&R sites, it is interesting how enigmatic these marks remain to archaeologists, who have no consensus of opinion regarding their significance. Celtic folk stories associate them with magical properties; to traditional people around the globe, hollows or holes in stones indicate sacred or supernatural characteristics. The curative power of rock is linked with spirits in rocks or in the Underworld/Otherworld; C&R marked rocks historically have been receivers of libations in honour of such spirits. In the Scottish Highlands, for example, the libations were of milk for fairies or guardian spirits.

C&R marks are Neolithically associated with burial sites, standing stones, and astronomical alignments. C&R carvings in Switzerland are similar to those in Galicia and in Scotland, reinforcing suspicion of a "proto-Celtic" connection. Globally, cup-marks date from at least the Upper Palaeolithic to the present day. Atlantic rock art appeared in the 4th century BCE. Argyll rock art seems to have been created during two different phases: earlier concentric circles and double spirals (also seen in Orkney passage-graves) and later cup-and-rings, many of them breached by a radial line. Open-air rock art was in use over a much longer period of time than that created for tombs. Coming upon a C&R mark, one may still feel the urge to place something – liquid, pebbles, flowers – into cup-marks on horizontal surfaces. But these carvings also occur on vertical and even overhanging surfaces. What strikes me, seeing them, is a cup-mark's resemblance to an inverted cairn, and a cup-and-ring's resemblance to an inverted cairn-henge.

Achnabreck Rock Art

Just north of Lochgilphead, signposted on the right; forestry road leading to the car park and trailhead. (NR 856 907)

At the Achnabreck car park, hike up the trail through a forestry plantation (largely deforested when we visited) to Scotland's largest concentration of rock art. These carvings date from the mid-4th millennium BCE to about 1000 BCE, and cover three glaciated outcrops grouped on one hillside. The carvings are cut into the living rock above Glen Crinan and Strathmartin, looking south and west to Loch Gilp and Loch Fyne.

The art is made up of cup-and-ring marks, many of them multi-ringed and breached with radial lines. But there are also networks of grooves, spirals, multiple rings without cups, and cups without rings. The designs are abstract yet evocative – but of what? In their groups the carvings are almost unsettling. They remind me of Aboriginal Dreamtime landscapes or sacred maps. Looking at them, are we the big looking at the small – god's-eye view, aerial perspective – or are we the small looking at the big – wee humans envisioning the universe? Or both? Neither? Are these records of celestial events? Doors and passages in and out of the Otherworld? Circles and paths of labyrinths; the womb; birth and death?

Each section of the rock art, although having much in common with its neighbours, appears to have a "speciality." For example, on the first section – Lower Achnabreck – are very large rings and multiple concentric rings with anything up to seven orbits. The next site – Middle Achnabreck – has one of the largest cup-and-ring carvings found anywhere in Scotland. This is some 3'2" in diameter and has seven orbits. The third section – with the imaginative name of Upper Achnabreck – has an emphasis on grooves or gutters, and enclosures that group certain cups and rings together. The grooves usually project radially from a central cupmark to meet or even cut outer circles. Some grooves continue through the rings for some inches, or even feet, before terminating on "open" slab.

Upper Achnabreck has some very interesting engravings rarely encountered elsewhere. There are two double-spirals and one triple-spiral. The triple is thought to be significantly older than other markings on the rocks. As with cairns, earlier Neolithic work is often the most complex. A matching pair of double-spirals is found among the Palaeolithic carvings of Lianyungang in the Jiangsu Province of eastern China. The style, either in this complex form or in single spirals, is also found in the rock art of American Indians, Australian Aboriginal work, and in Central Asian carvings and symbolism.

Cairnbaan

Backtrack slightly toward Lochgilphead; Cairnbaan is signposted on the right as you go south. (NR 838 910)

A closer echo of Australian Aboriginal and Palaeolithic Chinese rock art may be found across the strath from Achnabreck. Cairnbaan's cairn lies low on a slope to the south of the Crinan Canal; our destination, however, is not the cairn, but the rock art on the high ground to the north. Park at the foot of the hill; the walk to the decorated outcrops is not long but is assuredly uphill. Reward is the view from the top, and the art, similar in both respects to

Achnabreck, though neither view nor art is as extensive as at Achnabreck. Two sites comprise Cairnbaan, both full of cups and rings, meandering grooves, and a particularly striking design with conjoined multiple rings. None of this fancy spiral stuff here, but rather an emphasis on grooves and gutters – or looked at another way – an emphasis on connectivity. Usage of the term "gutter" is not without justification: on each slab many of the grooves do in fact run in the same (more of less) direction and, in some cases, this corresponds with the gradient of the slab, suggesting motion or flow.

 Motion and flow are clearly seen in a climate such as Scotland's. Rainwater gathering in cups, running along the gutters, sometimes filling the encircling rings. Motion is also implied in the spirals, like whirlpools. Europe's second largest whirlpool, the Corryvreckan, is found not far from Cairnbaan. The sound of it at ebb and flow thunders across the land. Its clockwise and counterclockwise eddies are reflected in the carvings

Another rock art site is at **Kilmichael Glassary** (NR 863 945).

Dunadd

North from Lochgilphead on the Kilmartin road. (NR 837 935). Signposted on the left. Car park and easy access (uphill path).

The hillfort at Dunadd, on an isolated knoll in the midst of open fields, is a Celtic rather than Neolithic site.[2] Its fame comes from its stint (500-800 AD) as a Dal Riatan stronghold. The Dal Riatans were early Irish settlers in Argyll; Iron Age Celts. On one of Dunadd's upper tiers is a smooth rock outcrop distinguished by a stone footprint, stone basin, Ogham inscriptions, and a carving of a

---

[2] Celtic languages form the basis of a large number of **place-names in Scotland**, particularly in the Highlands. Some names have Pictish roots; many are Gaelic or anglicised from the Gaelic. Some, especially in the Hebrides and Northern Isles, have Norse links. Gaelic placenames are wonderfully descriptive -- to learn the meaning is to become intimate with a place or land-feature. Road signs in some areas of the Highlands and Islands are bilingual, in Gaelic and English.

boar – perhaps relating to the Pictish king Angus I, and suggestive of a Dal Riatan-Pictish alliance. This inscribed outcrop overlooking a panorama of the valley's verdant invitation, and visible from the sites of 14 hillforts surrounding Dunadd, is where Scotland's first Celtic kings were inaugurated by placing a foot into the print in the living stone.

Kilmartin

Continue north from Dunadd; sites are signposted on the left as you approach and enter Kilmartin.

The Kilmartin valley – Strathmartin – hosts an amazing complex of monuments. The strath is recognized as having been an important ritual landscape for a period of at least 2000 years. Burial practices during Kilmartin's ceremonial era shifted from Neolithic communal tombs to Bronze Age individual cists, but the older communal tombs retained their sanctity throughout both ages, as can be seen from their focal placement amid newer cairns. It is probable that the concentration of monuments in Kilmartin served people of a much larger catchment area; it is apparent that mid-Argyll was a region of social stability and material as well as spiritual wealth. The earliest settlements in Kilmartin were already established by 7000 BCE, and farming took hold after 4000 BCE with an influx of new settlers.

The main Kilmartin sites are easily found and accessed, often situated in view of one another, and well marked by road and trail signs. Mid-Argyll has literally hundreds of monuments; only the primary ones have been developed with signage and car parks, so if you get tired of manicured displays, get an Ordnance Survey map and go explore. A 1961-2 field survey lists 639 historic and prehistoric monuments in mid-Argyll alone.

But returning to the signposted Kilmartin complex, the first of the main sites encountered (as you come north from Dunadd) is the ***Dunchraigaig*** (Fort of the Crag) Cairn (NR 833 968), a grassy mound of stones with several cists inside. I don't know if there were trees around Dunchraigaig when the cairn was in use, but their sheltering proximity now gives the place a graceful, sympathetic atmosphere.

The cairn is estimated to have exceeded 30 metres in diameter. On the southeastern side of the cairn is a cist with an enormous capping stone, aligned NE-SW. This was excavated circa 1864 and was found to contain cremated and uncremated remains of eight to ten individuals, each deposit of remains separated from the others by stone. Just to the north of centre is another cist, ENE-WSW, which contained a food vessel, flints, and some cremated remains. Beneath a rough basal paving, the excavating team discovered a "crouched burial" with its head oriented to the northeast. There was a third cist, oriented NE-SW, containing cremated remains, though this cist can no longer be seen.

Walking northwest through the trees, cross a stream into an open field and, continuing, come to the cup-and-ring engraved slabs of *Baluachraig*. (NR 831 969) The art is on a large glaciated slab breaking a surface of clipped grass. Beyond is a spring-fed wetlands that may have related to the choice of location of the art. Dozens of C&R markings adorn the outcrop – a wonderful sight. It is interesting to note that rock art designs are identical in Argyll, Orkney, and Ireland.

Walking back to Dunchraigaig and beyond, there is a path into the open field where the six tall **Ballymeanoch** (Middle Township) stones stand in an unusual 2-line formation, and visual prospects expand. (NR 833 964) Among these stones comprising two lines of monoliths arranged NW-SE, is what may be the most decorated standing stone in Scotland. The six monoliths are in two parallel lines, one of four stones, the remaining two a short distance to the southwest. There once was a seventh stone standing northwest of the two-stone line. The tallest of the six present stones in almost 14' in height; these are slabs with the emaciated profiles of fashion models, some of them leaning as though whispering with their neighbours.

Sitting by the first line of stones, contemplating the facing pair of stones, I was intrigued by how different this seemed from the effect created by a circle. While I was musing on Neolithic configurations, my companion literally stumbled across a fragment of the "missing" seventh stone, in a drainage ditch close to the nearby Ballymeanoch Cairn. He scraped grass and earth from the surface and only then realized what he was looking at.

This seventh stone was remarkable. By early accounts, it had been placed as a solitary outlier, its long axis perpendicular both to the lines of other stones, and to the individual orientations of those stones, i.e. it presented its broadest faces to the direction the lines indicate. But even more intriguingly, the stone is heavily cup-marked and has a fist-sized hole cut all the way through the slab.

According to descriptions of the Ballymeanoch Stone lines, sighting along the 4-stone group in the northwest direction, shows the point where the midwinter full moon will set at the major lunar standstill. (See the appendix for astronomical diagrams.) If this orientation is reversed, the southeast sighting is the point where the sun will rise at winter solstice.

Looking southeast along the line of the 2-stone group, pinpoints the most southerly moon rise at the major lunar standstill. The 4-stone group is height gradated, increasing toward the southeast, perhaps suggesting the relative importance of this lunar phenomenon.

The two central stones of the 4-group are both heavily decorated with cupmarks, but each stone is engraved on only one face – one on its east side and one on its west face.

The stone lines are only the beginning of what is to be found in that grassy field. *The Bally-meanoch Henge* lies 150 metres SSW of the standing stones. It is classically formed with an outer bank encircling a ditch. Causeways enter the inner space at the NE and SW. Roughly 40m in diameter, the henge contain two cists, both still visible. The central cist, oriented N-S, is constructed of large slabs and partially covered by a massive capping stone. At the time of the first excavation – by Greenwell in 1864 – the cist had been disturbed and nothing was found in it, only its pebbled floor. Slightly NE of this cist lies another, though only three stones now remain. This was excavated undisturbed and contained three inhumations, and beaker fragments.

Just 29m NE of the standing stones is the *kerb cairn* beside which my companion found the fragmented remains of the "seventh stone." The kerb cairn is about 7m in diameter – the drainage ditch has impinged. The remaining kerb stones, eleven in number, are size-gradated with the largest located on the SW side of the circle.

Lastly, there is an earth-work barrow mound between the road and the henge monument, about 30m in diameter and under 2m in height. This barrow was excavated in 1928, and although boulders and charcoal were discovered, no trace of any cist structures or burials was evident.

Back to the car park and proceeding up the road toward the village of Kilmartin, the next stop is at *Lady Glassery Wood*, signposted. In this field is a beautiful assembly of stones apparently aligned as a lunar observatory. The site is known as *Nether Largie Stones* (NR 827 978) and consists of four groupings on an approximate NE-SW axis. The long axis of the five largest stones – all are nearly 10' in height – is aligned roughly NNW-SSE. The single large central stone has about 40 cup-marks and other artwork on its SW face, and there is artwork on two of the outer stones.

The placement of these stones is such that the most northerly and most southerly positions of the moon at the major lunar standstill are indicated. From another viewpoint, the stones indicate the most northerly setting of the full moon, and from yet another, the southerly setting of the full moon. By standing at the southernmost pairing and looking northwest, the observer sees the extreme northern setting position of the full moon at the major standstill. If the observer sights from the north-eastern most stone, the line of sight is directed to the setting full moon at its extreme southern extent.

Whether any of this was intended, we do not know, but it has been suggested that this site constitutes one of the most important (Neolithic) lunar sites in Scotland.

Like a Neolithic theme park, Kilmartin really packs it in. Two or three minutes on the footpath will take the visitor from the Nether Largie Stones to *Temple Wood*, (NR 827 979) also known as Half Moon Wood.

The northeast circle at Temple Wood evolved through many phases of construction, and was originally built of timber posts (thus its name), that were replaced by stones even before all the intended posts had been erected. But even the stone version may never have been completed. The southwest companion to this circle, with its cists and cairns, seems to have become the site's main focus. Building activity at the site went on until 3000 BCE and the site was in use until 1050 BCE, with usage changing from ritual to funerary over that period.

Temple Wood's two circles, aligned on a SW-NE axis, are watched over by a grove of lovely old trees overlooking the circles. It gives perspective: human duration ephemeral beside the trees, who are ephemeral beside a stone site whose status has spanned five and a half millennia.

The simpler NE circle, at first sight, consists of a flattened disc of smallish cobbles with a few small kerb stones – possibly small uprights – just within the perimeter. A single upright stone used to mark the centre. Actually the configuration is slightly elliptical, 32'6" by 34'. Radiocarbon dating suggests that this site with its timber posts was originally constructed circa 3500 BCE making it one of the earliest projects in the UK.

The SW circle is considerably more complex, with three cists and concentric rings. The cobbled area is about 60' in diameter. The principle circle consists of a ring of low uprights, which lies within the cobbled disc and has a 40' diameter. The circle uprights, which are generally thin slabs of slatey shist, are arranged with their long axes parallel to the circumference of the circle – except for one. A stone in the SE arc is actually set perpendicular to the circumference. Two of the stones – on the north and NE of the arc – are decorated with rock art: the northmost stone has linked spirals engraved across two faces, one spiral clockwise, the other counter; on the outer face of the NE decorated stone is a single engraving of concentric circles, though this is very faint – so faint that only the sensitivity of fingertips confirms its existence.

In the interior of this circle are three cists all following the NE-SW orientation of the two greater circles. There is also a small kerbed cairn slightly off-centre, with a NE bias within the greater circle.

Temple Wood reminded me of Aberdeenshire's Easter Aquorthies circle in its pristine – bordering on sterile – presentation, though both sites are worthy of great appreciation. What touched me most about Temple Wood was that the SW circle's cist was a child's grave.

From Temple Wood, wander over to the unique linear cemetery of five cairns, (NR 828 979), which was developed over a thousand-year span and was actively used from 3000 BCE to 1200 BCE. The line of Clyde-style cairns orients SSW-NNE. Closest to Temple Wood is the oldest of the cairns, *Nether Largie South*. The great burial mound of Nether Largie South is the central cairn in the linear cemetery. Some of these cairns are separated by little more than 200 yards, some slightly further, but none are distant. Although each cairn has its own unique qualities, including much rock art, the galleried chamber of Nether Largie South sets it apart.

This is probably the earliest cairn in the series. It has a vaguely egg-shaped plan of approximately 34m by 27m with a height of 4½m, with the narrower end pointing northeast. Plundering of stones for farm walls, drains, and roads has reduced the height and form of the cairn.

The centrally located chamber aligns NE-SW with the entrance at the NE. Huge slabs and drystone walling constitute the 6.1m by 1.9m by 0.8m chamber, which is subdivided into four compartments by upright slabs. A very skillful construction.

In the SW compartment, a small cist of slabs and capstone was discovered. By the time of Greenwell's excavation, the cist had already been disturbed, but Greenwell assumed that the scattered fragments of beaker pottery and unburned bones constituted the original contents. A little further to the northern end of this compartment a slab was found to cover a cremation deposit. Digging revealed that a pavement of pebbles had been laid down the centre of the compartment, delimited at either end by stone slabs. Beneath the pebbles was further evidence of cremation burial. Flint arrowheads, and a cow or bull's tooth were found along with ubiquitous broken quartz pebbles. Beneath this layer, yet another pavement had been constructed. A similar stratification of pebble pavement and burial remains was found in the next compartment, which also contained fragments of Beakerware.

Two other cists were embedded within the matrix of the cairn. In one was a food vessel; the second was empty.

The interior of the chamber brings Maes Howe to mind. Although this one is much simpler in design and has suffered more from the ravages of time and robbers, a wholeness of atmosphere curiously remains. Creativity is in evidence, the qualities that the builders
brought to, and left behind, in this work. Something that was and is greater than the sum of its parts.

The next cairn to the NNE up the line is *Nether Largie Mid*, and much of its height has been reduced as stones were removed for road repair purposes. Unlike the older Nether Largie South, this cairn contained individual cists instead of a chambered tomb. One of the cists is visible near the south edge of the cairn; the other is hidden. Both were empty when excavated. A cup-mark and a carved axehead on the inner surface of one of the cist slabs remains, and cup-marks on another slab to the northeast of the cist.

Nether Largie North is next; this cairn is a strange set-up. The entire cairn was removed during excavation in 1930, then rebuilt – with disconcerting modifications. In the re-constructed cairn's centre is a large cist aligned N-S, set into a pit. The cist is viewed by climbing down modern steps into a concrete bunker the roof of which is set with a rectangle of translucent tiles permitting natural light. An interesting ambience. But the cist lid declares prehistoric reality; it is a heavy capstone adorned with around forty cup-marks and ten carved axeheads.

Glebe Cairn is at the northern end of the linear cemetery, and may as well be viewed from the road (the cairn is behind the Kilmartin Museum) as from nearby, as all there is to see now is a large reconstructed heap of stones. The two concentric boulder-rings that once distinguished the cairn's southwest quadrant (which contained a cist) are no longer extant, nor is the cairn's interior cist.

Ri Cruin, at the opposite end of the linear cemetery, has more to recommend it. For one, its location within a pleasing grove of trees. But this cairn too is largely a reconstruction. Three cists are visible, one of them having a decorated slab end, though this too is a reconstruction, not the original.

Kilmartin village is tiny but has its attractions: the small but fine museum and shop; exemplary B&Bs; and a pub that serves sustaining food and drink — and has a pool table.

Ford Digression

Travelling north from Kilmartin on the A816, turn right onto the single-track road leading to Ford, at the southwest end of Loch Awe.

When Tolkien wrote about the Shire, he may have had in mind a place like the short strath that lies between the A816 and the Loch Awe-side village of Ford,[3] a crease of land nestling among

---

[3] Navigating, on Scottish roads, can be as challenging as driving on them. The roads are not well marked in terms of route numbers or cardinal directions; town/village names are often the indicators of which road to take. The wise thing,

and between craggy knolls, beside the rills of myriad waters. Oak, rowan, and birch are earthed in luxuriously moist cushions of flamboyant moss. The riverside flats are walled and grazed; jagged upthrusts of land dominate – higher, rockier levels too nutrient-poor to sustain much more that the occasional scrub tree. The single-track road's narrowness is emphasized by dry-stone walls tight to either side, as the road winds between pastures themselves squeezed between rugged knolls and patrician walls.

This geography, that determined the course of the road, also dictated the locations for Neolithic industry; almost every monument in this strath is a roadside attraction. These sites are not signposted or developed, so if driving up this road, do so slowly and keep looking around – none of the monuments are far off.

---

therefore, is to check ahead on your map, for the names in the direction in which you hope to go. **Ordinance Survey maps** (OS maps), available in shops and tourist offices, can be a huge help in navigating as well as in discovering an area's hidden wonders. Allow plenty of journey time for driving on rural roads.

The first site, **Glennan**, (NM 857 012) is on the right, and comprises two cairns and a standing stone. The monument is in an accessible pasture where cows often graze, and is shaded in part by an open stand of mature hardwoods. Both cairns are only a few yards from the dry-stone wall. The more northerly, larger cairn has a diameter of 37'4" and a height of 4'10". The centres of both cairns have been disturbed, and the cover stone of the larger cairn has been exposed. This slab, roughly 5'2" by 4', displays at least nine cup-marks. There is some evidence that a ditch may once have surrounded this cairn.

The second cairn, about ten feet SSW from the first, is similarly shaped but lacks the elaborate cist slab.

The site's standing stone is about 100 yards beyond the cairns, east into the field. The stone is embedded in the ruined stonework of a derelict farm building. Whether the building was constructed around the stone, or the stone "poached" from another location I wouldn't care to guess, but the fact that it appears to be aligned NNE-SSW, a similar orientation to that of the twin cairns, suggests that it remains where it was initially raised. The stone is a little over 7' in height, tapering to a slender pinnacle.

The next menhir along this road also stands immediately east (on the right) as you travel toward Ford. This is known as the ***Creagantairbh Stone*** (Stone of the Bull) (NM 859 016) and tragically is broken. Had it not sheered it would be one of the tallest monoliths in Scotland. What is left of it, embedded in its original E-W alignment, still attains a height of 5'10". The broken section lying just east of the stump is over 10' in length, so the stone must have towered a little over 16' before succumbing to a gale in 1879. Looking at the massive remains, I'm glad I missed that storm.

Following the western line of sight from this stone, the view is checked by Am Barr, one of the small but steep-sided knolls crowding in on this snug strath. There are a couple theories about this line of sight. One is that it could have marked a stellar line – the declination is consistent with that of the Pleiades circa 2600 BCE. Alternately, it could have pointed directly to the sunset at March and September equinoxes.

Kintraw

> From the Ford digression, backtrack to the A816 and proceed a very brief distance north; the monument is immediately on the right. (NM 830 050)

Above and just south of the head of Loch Craignish stands the stunning Kintraw monument. You can't get more accessible than this – it is barely off the road. The site lies at the entrance to the Bealach Mor – the Great pass – and occupies a terrace with a commanding view toward the southwest. Crowded together on the terrace are cairns, an enclosure, and a soaring standing stone.

The larger cairn, about 48' in diameter and some 7' in height, is surrounded by kerb stones gradated to the south and west. On the southwest periphery is a so-called "false portal" that looks like a 3-sided open-topped cist fronted by a recumbent block. Once again, quartz pebbles were used during construction; in this case, distributed around the rim of the cairn. During excavations (1959-60 and 1979) a cist was uncovered with cremated bone fragments inside. Southwest of this cairn is a smaller kerb-cairn. Within the north-western perimeter, as with the larger cairn, was a cist. This one only contained carbonized wood.

    Between the two cairns is a standing stone 13' in height, though it seems much taller. The Kintraw monolith is a racy – dare I say phallic – stone of splendid grace. A cleft at its top may have been used to align with winter solstice sunsets between the distant hills known as the Paps (breasts) of Jura. The stone was originally aligned by profile in a NNE-SSW orientation but, following its collapse in 1979, it was re-set incorrectly.

    Alexander Thom suggested that using the stone as a back-sight for the winter solstice alignment would not work unless the original sighting and research was done from a platform some way up the steep hill behind the cairns, allowing an uninterrupted view. Sure enough, such a platform was found. Once the original positioning of the stone had been done, subsequent observations could be made by viewing past the monolith from the top of the larger cairn. Calculating the shift in the elliptic since Neolithic times, Thom dated the monolith circa 1800 BCE.

Further investigating of the site revealed yet another structure, 20 yards northwest of the standing stone. Here can be seen the very faint remains of an earth and stone enclosure of some 50' diameter. The raised banking averages 6'6" in breadth and, interestingly, in sketches of the site made by Edward Lhuyd in 1699, we can see a stone kerb within the banking, with four stones set externally. None of this remains today, but the site in its entirety is impressive.

Strontoiller Stone Circle

Continuing north from Kintraw on the A816, at Kilmore turn right, then left at the T-junction and proceed along Loch Nell, turning right to reach Strontoiller Farm. You really need an Ordnance Survey Map of the area, as neither roads nor circle are well signposted. (NM 907 289)

A casual glance at the map for this area – Lorne (Lathurna in Gaelic, named after either Ireland's Larne or King Fergus' sibling) – shows a wealth of Neolithic endeavour. As a single exemplar Strontoiller certainly does the trick. Within a small area are a stone circle, a kerb-cairn, and a standing stone. The latter two are adjacent to the single-track road, and the circle is barely 200 yards to the northwest.

The circle, consisting of rounded granite boulders, is low in height but densely packed – the northern arc is pretty much stone to stone to stone. There is a sizable gap to the south, looking toward

Loch Nell. The strange crowding and gaps give the circle a somewhat unruly appearance. The ring is about 65' in diameter and made up of 31 stones, the tallest of which is barely 3' in height.

The kerb-cairn, locally known as Diarmaid's Grave, is solidly kerbed with stones height-gradated toward the south. This cairn is compact and aesthetically pleasing. When it was excavated in 1967, cremated fragments of bone were found; also quartz pebbles evenly distributed throughout the cairn.

The cairn lies at the foot of Clach na Carraig (The Pinnacle Stone), a 13'4" giant. Not just tall, this substantial monolith has a surprisingly square cross-section, which, as an upright, makes it somewhat of an oddity. Lesser blocks than this were used as recumbent stones in circles in Aberdeen-shire.

From Strontoiller to Oban is another Ordnance Map adventure; roughly speaking, go back down the farm road, turning right, then left at Barranrioch, then left again into Oban, to catch the ferry to the Isle of Mull.

Additional Argyll Sites

- *Achnacree & Achnacreebeag Chambered Cairns* – Lorne (NM 922 363) Neolithic
- *Ballochroy Standing Stones & Cist* – Kintyre (NR 730 523) 3 standing stones, massive cist.
- *Corriechrevie Cairn* – Kintyre (NR 738 540)

Additional Sites on Argyll Islands

- Bute: *Ettrick Bay Stone Circle* (NS 044 668) Ring and outliers.
- Islay: *Ballinaby Standing Stones* (NR 219 672) 2 stones, 1 is very tall.
- *Kildalton Celtic Cross* (NR 458 508)
- *Cultoon Stone Circle* (NR 195 569) partially destroyed.
- Tiree: *Hough Stone Circle* (NL 959 451) 2 tumbled rings.
- *Dun Mor* (NM 042 492) Broch, well-preserved gallery.

- Lismore: *Tirefour Broch* (NM 867 429) magnificent position

Isle of Mull & the Road to Skye

The Isle of Mull is a scenic treat; an island even other Scots are addicted to visiting. Its interior is mountainous, its coast snakes in endless complexity. It is graced by woodlands – a premium in the isles – and intriguing basalt rock formations. Wildlife is plentiful, the weather moody, and Mull's capital. Tobermory, is a photogenic fishing port.

Mull was the seat of the MacLean clan; Duart Castle worth a detour to see. Mull was also the ancestral home of the MacKinnons. Places of interest to Mull visitors include Tobermory Distillery; MacCulloch's Fossil Tree; fascinating boat trips; and of course, Mull's solitary stone circle.[4]

The ferry crossing from Oban takes you to Craignure, on Mull's east coast. Buses service the

---

[4] **Staffa** is a small, uninhabited flat-topped island riddled with caves -- including the famous Fingal's Cave -- and is a primary nesting area for multitudes of puffins. The island's amazing hexagonal basalt columns, and the acoustic effects of the sea booming through its caverns, make Staffa hauntingly memorable. Boat trips to Staffa depart from Dervaig, Fionnphort, and Ulva Ferry. Boat trips to Ulva and the Treshnish Isles are also available.

island, but there are no Post Buses, so a private vehicle is essential for accessing Mull's stone circle and other out-of-the-way attractions. Island accommodations include B&Bs, hotels, cottages, camping, and a few hostels. The tourist industry is active on Mull, and the resident population is comprised far more of transplants than natives, Mull one of the places cleared of its indigenous people in the 19th century. It is an island of contrasts.

If taking a side trip to Iona, the visitor encounters some of Scotland's notable Celtic Crosses.[5] These are far more recent stone monuments than Neolithic circles; but in basic form, Celtic Crosses predate Christianity by at least 600 years. The earliest forms may've had geomantic connotations. But the Celtic Crosses seen in Scotland come mainly from the

---

[5] There are no stone circles on the island of **Iona**, off the Ros of Mull, but some of Scotland's Celtic Crosses originated and are still seen there. The island is reached by a short ferry crossing from Finnphort (foot passengers only) and is a lovely place to explore, having exquisite white beaches, curious rocks, emerald pastures, and much of historical interest. The famed Iona Abbey overlooks the burial place for kings.

5th to 9th centuries. The typical configuration combines a cross with a circle at the juncture of the arms, ornamented with interlace and fretwork openings.

Some of the ancient standing stones were Christianised by carving crosses or other Christian images on them. Celtic "high" crosses were freestanding, purpose-made from dressed stone, developed during the 8th and 9th centuries. During this period Pictish Symbol Stones began featuring crosses and Biblical scenes also. Traditionally Celtic Crosses were not used in conjunction with burial grounds, but today are often seen in cemetery memorials.

Loch Buie Stone Circle

Take the A849 south from Craignure to Strathcoil; turn left onto the single-track to Loch Buie. The circle is 13½ miles ENE of Bunessan, off the Lochbuie village side-road. Park and walk ½ mile across a level field. (NM 618 251)

My companion and I made our way to Loch Buie through pounding rain. It was June – lavish banks of rhododendrons bloomed along the single-track road. The approach to the circle and its outliers was, for us that day, a "welly-boot" excursion. But every cloud has a silver lining; the level sweep of the field, though not facilitating drainage, does allow the visitor to see one of the circle's outliers and the kerb-cairn, almost from the road. By following these beacons, the path to the major circle is easily found. Just keep in mind that the most direct approach is not always the most desirable.

The circle is in excellent shape, beautiful stones and beautiful setting, whatever the weather. The circle's location was once known as "The Field of the Druids" and while that may be a fanciful 19th century appellation, the place does evoke an otherworldly mood. The circle, set in a small field surrounded by thickets of rhododendron, has been preserved to a remarkable extent. The 44' ring is constructed of good-sized stones. Only one stone is not original – the stone to the north. The survivors have weathered the millennia well. The tallest stone of the circle (WSW) is 6'3" in height, but this is by no means the tallest stone of the wider monument; to the southwest stands a magnificent 9'4" monolith. It may not be significant, but a line extended from the centre of the circle and grazing the shoulder of that tall WSW stone, points toward a coastal cairn to the south of Loch Buie village.

Less than 300 yards northwest of the circle, in a leafy copse where sheep were sheltering from the downpour the day of our visit, we came upon the remnants of a *kerb-circle*. Like some of the small rings seen in Argyll, this one has a "false portal" at the southeast. This ring's ruined state among tree roots – its hidden-ness in this copse – made the tumbled stones seem all the more mysterious. The cairn's orientation suggests an association with winter solstice.

We emerged from the trees and were continuing back across the saturated field when my companion spotted the Loch Buie circle's fourth outlier. Isolated 400 yards NNW of the main circle, the 6½' tall monolith adamantly gestures towards Gleann a' Chraiginn Mhòir, the only northern pass through the mountains.

Additional Mull Sites
Ardnacross Standing Stones & Cairns
- On a hillside terrace to the WSW of Ardnacross Farm. (NM 542 491)
- *Date of Construction*: Possibly from the 2nd half of the 2nd millennium BCE.
- *Configuration*: A group of 3 small kerbed cairns between 2 parallel lines of stones – only 1 is still upright. Another kerb-cairn lies to the NNW of the farm.

Dervaig Standing Stones
- Three separate alignments, NE, E, and SE of the village of Dervaig.
- *Configurations*: There are 3 upright and 1 fallen stone in a forest clearing on Maol Mor

(NM 435 531); there are 5 stones (2 upright) in a small clearing on the north side of the Dervaig-Tobermory road (NM 439 520); there are 3 low stones about 850 metres ESE of Dervaig on the south side of the road. (NM 438 516)

The Road to Skye

There are many options travelling from Mull to Skye. If not going by private vehicle, the best bet is to return to Oban and travel by train to Mallaig and the ferry to Skye. If driving from Mull, however, the choices mainly depend on how fast you want to go and how fond you are of single-track driving. All the routes are scenic.

There is the Tobermory-Kilchoan crossing to Ardnamurchan and through Moidart and Morar; there is the Fishnish-Lochaline crossing into Moidart and Morar; both of these routes involve a fair amount of single-track driving. And there is the Criagnure-Oban crossing to the main road to Skye.

Since this is the most often chosen, I'll describe it in detail.

From Oban, take the A85 north to the A828 north. An interesting stop is at **Dunstaffnage Castle**, just south of the Falls of Lora at the mouth of Loch Etive. The castle was once held by Clan Alpin, and indeed it is here that the Stone of Destiny was kept. Over the centuries Clan Alpin lost the castle and it became the seat of the Lorne clan MacDougall.

Not much further on is a reminder of more recent history; **Barcaldine Castle**, not visible from the road, was the location of treachery when in the winter of 1691 MacIain of Glencoe was held at this castle to prevent his reaching Inverary in time to sign an oath of allegiance to King William. This "delayed" arrival at the capital town of Argyll ultimately resulted in the massacre of Glencoe.

South of Glenachulish, a little before the village of Duror, can be glimpsed an older and perhaps less cruel history. A solitary tall monolith keeps watch over the settlement – and the road traffic – marking a Neolithic site of some significance. The local church, **Keil**, which dates from the medieval period, was dedicated to Colm Cille – St. Columba – suggesting that the site was chosen in recognition of pre-existing, pre-Christian, spiritual importance.

Nearing the Ballachulish Bridge, take the A82 toward Fort William, though a side-trip the other way, to *Glencoe*, is highly recommended if you have time. At the south end of the Ballachulish Bridge, on the rocky knoll just west of the road, stands the monument for *James of the Glen*, executed in 1752 following a farcical trial and legendary miscarriage of justice. Sentenced to death for the murder of Colin Campbell of Glenure, James' bones swung on the gibbet for years following the hanging, as a warning to uppity Highlanders.

Reaching Fort William and its series of roundabouts (traffic circles, not stone circles), stay with the A82, or signs for Inverness. Once beyond Fort William you will be presented with another choice: either the shorter route (a left onto the

A830) to Mallaig and the ferry to Skye; or continuing on the A82 through Spean Bridge to Invergarry, where you turn left (west) onto the A87. Then proceed to a T-junction where you turn left (west) again on the A87, through magnificent *Glen Shiel*, Shiel Bridge, Inverinate, along Loch Duich to Dornie and *Eilean Donan Castle* (the most photographed castle in Scotland and the set for a number of films) to Kyle of Lochalsh and the *Skye Bridge* – now toll-free.

A side trip to visit the brochs of Glenelg[6] is recommended. Turn left at the Shiel Bridge sign for the scenic route (and ferry to Skye). This single-track road climbs the magnificent Ratagan Pass – breathtaking views over Loch Duich. Continue through the village of Glenelg, following signs to the brochs in their lovely leafy setting. **Dun Trod-**

---

[6] **Brochs** are Iron Age fortified homesteads unique to Scotland. They are tall, circular, drystone towers overlooking the sea or small glens. Their thick stone walls are hollow, with internal stairways leading to upper galleries. The brochs' central courtyards are circular, often with rooms leading off, within the walls. Scotland's hundreds of brochs are mainly found in Caithness, Sutherland, the Northern Isles, and the west coast and its islands.

dan (NG 883 172) and **Dun Telve** (NG 829 172) are two of Scotland's best examples of broch construction. There is also, in summer months (Easter – October), the Glenelg ferry to Kylerhea, on Skye, a six-minute crossing.

If you instead choose the A830 when beyond Fort William, you'll have a shorter and perhaps even more scenic journey than that through Glen Shiel, but will be dependent on ferry timetables. The road to Mallaig takes you past **Glenfinnon** with its Highlander monument at the head of Loch Shiel, and the Glenfinnon railway viaduct that Harry Potter fans will recognize from the films. The road continues through rocky hills and beside glimmering lochs, classic West Coast countryside, to the inviting *sands of Morar*, and road's end at the fishing port of *Mallaig*, and the 20 minute ferry crossing to Skye.

The Isle of Skye

Skye is a big island with a big landscape, 50 miles from end to end, with a deeply indented coast; nowhere on Skye are you more than 5 miles from the sea. A magnificent island; the Cuillin – the powerful range of mountains at its heart – is like a craggy kingdom heaved sheer from the sea. Each of the island's peninsulas has its own weather, scenery, and cultural flavour: many islands in one.

There are castles with gardens and visitor centres at either end of Skye – *Armadale's clan Donald complex and Museum of the Isles; and Dunvegan's MacLeod castle and gardens.*[7] There are wonderful boat trips to outlying islands – Rum, Eigg, Muck, and Canna – and a ferry to the stunning Isle of Rasaay; boat excursions to view seals,

---

[7] A scenic side trip to enjoy is a drive or bus ride to *Talisker Distillery* in the village of Carbost. To reach this famed whisky centre, turn onto the A863 – the Dunvegan road – off the A87 at Sligachan, and go left onto the single-track B8009 along Loch Harport to Carbost. Just up the road from Carbost is the village of Portnalong which was re-populated by Gaels from the islands of Lewis and Harris after World War I, and still has a population of native speakers.

whales and the undersea world; superb walks, superb whisky; multitudes of hotels, B&Bs, hostels, cottages, a few campgrounds; and some of Scotland's finest restaurants. There are caves and pinnacles, cliffs and moors, and the world's only Gaelic-medium college, which is also the venue for world-class music and cultural events. Skye has a network of bus and PostBus routes. The island's capital is the village of Portree; there are banking and medical facilities there as well as in the village of Broadford; and Internet services also.

If arriving on Skye from the bridge, continue north on the A87 to the village of Broadford, and turn left onto the B8083 – the single-track to Elgol. If coming to Skye by the ferry from Mallaig to Armadale, follow the A851, the main Sleat road, to the T-junction, and turn left onto the A87 into Broadford, then left onto the Elgol road.

The single-track to Elgol winds through the beautiful peninsula of Strathaird and has many points of interest. We'll start with the stone circle and work our way back to Broadford.

Na Clachan Bhreige

Near Kilmarie, 7-8 miles SW of Broadford, off the Elgol road. (NG 543 176) Not signposted – the circle can be barely discerned from the road, on the right as you approach the Coruisk trailhead car park. Half-mile walk.

There are a number of cairns, duns, and brochs on Skye, some standing stones and symbol stones, but only one remaining stone circle. Na Clachan Bhreige – The False (or Lying) Men – according to local tradition, are the remains of a group of men who were turned to stone.

My companion and I first visited Na Clachan Bhreige on an overcast but dry morning. The same could not be said of the footing on the half-mile walk from road to site. I nearly lost a welly-boot in one sucking bog out of which my companion hauled me like a mired cow. Amid this terrain with its heather, snaking burns, and cairn-like humps, the stones stand pale grey as the overcast sky. Almost islanded now by water, there's no doubt this site used to be drier – one of the circle's remaining stones leans alarmingly in the saturated ground.

This is a monument easily overlooked, though – for the sharp-eyed – visible from the road. Having only three remaining stones, with no signage or path to drew attention, and dwarfed in the broad bowl of hills, the circle does not proclaim itself.

The circle – approaching 22' in diameter – is situated on the western banks of the small loch. Not recorded on maps dating from the early 1900s, the loch is actually the result of a small dam on the river. Unfortunately, as we discovered, this renders access to the site a wee bit soft.

Only three white quartz-rose stones (of 1.5, 2, and 1.8 metres in height) remain of a theoretically eight-stone ring. The survivors form a short arc from the WNW through N to ENE. Professor Alexander Thom (1894-1985) reports having probed the site, finding five other stones buried in the peaty soil. Other sources report the existence of a 3.5 metre prostrated pillar of reddish stone lying to the south. None of these additional stones are in evidence today. A small pestle-shaped object of polished black stone was recovered from the centre of the circle during the excavations of 1860.

Leaving this site, either continue on the Elgol road to Elgol itself and one of the island's best views of the Cuillin, or backtrack toward Broadford, making some stops along the way.[8] First

---

[8] In **crofting areas**, which Skye has in abundance, drivers have to contend with sheep (and sometimes cows) in the road. Be alert -- especially during lambing season and the summer months! Livestock will not necessarily vacate the road even if you toot your horn, and lambs in particular are prone to darting across the road if startled or separated from their

is the Neolithic chambered cairn at Kilmarie, reached by turning right onto a sidetrack signposted for the cemetery beyond Kilmarie House. (NG 553 173)

The cairn's name, **Cnocan nan Gobhar** (Hillock of the Goats) is apt: goat-like agility is needed to clamber up its steep sides, which are overgrown with moss and brambles, the rock prone to dislodgement; the side with the cairn's entrance drops sharply to the brisk
rocky riverbed just one nasty, bone-breaking slip away. To reach the cairn, park near Kilmarie House and cross the footbridge; the cairn can be seen even before reaching the bridge, as its entrance faces across the river. Once attaining the cairn's entrance, peek into the dark slab-sided recess and ponder the effort required to construct such a cairn on its riverside perch.

My companion and I walked downriver from the cairn, passing Kilmarie House on the

---

mothers. If a flock or herd is being moved along the road by a crofter, be patient. Don't try to bull through; don't honk. The crofter most likely will indicate when and where to pass.

opposite bank and continuing to the shore. We wandered up a slope above the shore, to a rocky headland surrounded by cliffs, where the ruins of **Dun Ringil** (NG 561 170) are moulded to the usual dramatic Celtic setting. The dun used to be a fortress of the MacKinnon clan.

The next stop on the return to Broadford is in the township of Kilbride (Brigid's Church) to visit its lone standing stone, **Clach na h-Annait** (The Stone of the Church). Turn right onto the Kilbride single-track; the standing stone is on the right, at the farm. (NG 590 205) Park by the road and walk down the drive to get a better look, or ask permission at the farm to examine the stone up close.

The pillar is almost eight feet tall, slim and austere. About fifty feet south of the stone is a holy well. There used to be a stone circle here also. By 1903 the circle, perhaps too confronting to the Christian congregation, had been dismantled. The entire site was taken over by the church at a fairly early date – a frequent fate for pagan sacred sites.

That the stone was given a Gaelic name connecting it with the church suggests that the stone was adopted into the local theological fold. Still, it looks proudly pagan.

On the right, as you continue toward Broadford, is the hillside concealing **High Pasture Cave**, currently an excavation site of considerable archaeological interest.

Finally on this Strath excursion, just before reaching Broadford, is **An Sithean**, The Fairy Hill, (NG 627 221) with its ruined cairn. More sheep than fairies are usually in evidence, but it is an enticing spot with its views of Beinn na Caillich and the lovely spread of countryside down Strath Suardal. There are so many suggestive outcrops and rocks littered about An Sithean, and the once chambered cairn is so dispersed, that it is difficult to make a clear distinction between structure and landscape – which is not a complaint. The cairn plainly exists, though its precise encompassment is vague.

You can see (or may have stopped at) the ruined *Cill Chriosd* church. (NG 617 207) There is evidence suggesting that the churchyard may have been a prehistoric burial site, later Christianised. Even its Christian pedigree is old, going back at least to the 1500s. Reputedly there was/is a stone circle beside the loch at Cill Chriosd. The loch was said to have been haunted by a monster at one time.

In the village of Broadford itself is the well-hidden **Liveras Chambered Cairn**, (NG 643 238) along the shore road near the pier. The cairn is disguised as a tree-covered uneven mound wedged between two houses. The houses are tight to each side of the cairn, the road is right in front. There is no signage, no cairn-like features; and *trees* on it, for goodness sakes.

It is as though the cairn is invisible. It was excavated in the 1800s, but archaeologists abandoned it mid-exploration, reportedly because of ghostly interference. The 14'x9'x6' high chamber was later accidentally discovered by a 9-year old girl, and artifacts such as an urn, stone wrist-guards, and several skulls were removed.

Additional Sites on Skye[9]

- *Borve Stone Row* – NW Skye (NG 452 480) 3 larger, 4 smaller stones, Bronze Age.
- *Kensaleyre Standing Stones* – Trotternish (NG 415 525) 2 lochside stones, Bronze Age.
- *Rudh an Dunain Cairns* – Central Skye (NG 393 163) Neolithic chambered cairn, Bronze and Iron Age remains.

Brochs:

---

[9] One of Skye's most dramatic landscapes can be admired on the loop road around the peninsula of **Trotternish**, in the island's north. From Portree, take the Staffin road -- the A855 -- up the coast past the Old Man of Storr pinnacle, Lealt Falls, Kilt Rock, and the dinosaur fossil museum. Some of this route is single-track, some double. From just north of Staffin either cut across the peninsula to the ferry port of Uig, or continue on the A855 past Flodigarry and the extraordinary rock formations of the Quiraing, to the Duntulm Castle ruins, the Museum of Island Life, views of the Outer Isles, and on to Uig. The drive from Uig to Portree on the A87 is less dramatic but includes Neolithic, Bronze Age, and Pictish standing stones and cairns.

- *Dun Beag* (NG 339 386) Well preserved, fine views.
- *Dun Ardtreck* (NG 335 358) Semi-broch.
- *Dun Fiadgairt* (NG 231 504) Unusual 2-entrance.
- *Dun Borrafiach* (NG 235 637) Scenic setting.
- *Dun Hallin* (NG 256 592) Well preserved, excellent vantage.

The Isle of Lewis is accessible by ferry from Skye. Embark at Uig, in Trotternish (at the north end of the island). The ferry journey takes about 2½ hours. Disembark at Tarbert, which is actually on the Isle of Harris. Harris – though a separate place – is not a separate landmass from Lewis.

The Western Isles

The Western Isles, also called the Outer Hebrides or the "Long Isle," is a chain of islands about 130 miles long. The only town of size is Stornoway, on the Isle of Lewis, which has an airport and ferry pier and is a hub for bus transport. All the major islands are connected by ferries or causeways; several islands have airports.

Most of the terrain is a juxtaposition of moorland, peat bog, machair, rock (especially on the east coasts) and beautiful beaches (particularly on the west coasts). The highest ground is rugged North Harris, though there is a range of hills down the spine of South Uist as well. The islands are jewelled by lochs, scoured by gales, pounded by seas, and layered by human and geological history. Norse influence shows in many of the place names and surnames, but Gaelic is the local language, and all road signs are in Gaelic or are bilingual.

Neolithic farmers appeared in the Western Isles perhaps 1000 years before anywhere else in the UK. You feel, hear, and see a deep continuity in the Outer Isles, however besieged their populations have been by economic and social challenges. Travellers in the Western Isles look more to B&Bs and hostels than to an abundance of hotels.[10] There is a great deal to see and enjoy on these islands, and the best way to do it is with a relaxed pace and open mind. Our Neolithic tour will focus on the islands of Lewis and North Uist.

Calanais

Off the A858 12 miles west of Stornoway. (NB 213 330) From Tarbert (Harris) go north on the A859 to the cut-over (left turn) onto the A858. Well signposted and easily accessible.

---

[10] Western Isles hostels include the unique **"crofter's hostels"** which have fairly simple facilities: coal fires/storage heaters, bunks or camp beds, gas cookers, hot showers; and each is looked after by a crofter living nearby. No advance bookings are accepted. The hostel chain is run by a charitable organization -- the Gatliff Hebridean Hostels Trust at GHHT@peterclarke.com.

I first saw Calanais just a short while after the visitor centre was built. The centre is out of sight of the stones, designed to blend with the landscape. You walk up a short path from the centre, turn a corner, and – voila! – there are the stones.

Much of the Isle of Lewis is now peat bog. It didn't used to be this way. Over millennia peat engulfed a great deal of the Calanais monument; it wasn't until 1857 that the site was cleared to its original level. Calanais is elegant – graceful shapes and colours. The overall effect is a mineral dance troupe frozen in time. Strolling around the arrangement, perspective keeps changing, the choreography becoming more and more intricate and compelling.

Calanais is made from gneiss quarried perhaps a mile away. Beautiful grey blushed with feldspar pink striations and green-black hornblende clusters, the stones almost lithe in form. Gneiss is one of the earth's most ancient stones – three thousand million years old. Holding a continuous memory of our planet almost from its birth. Gazing at the Calanais stones you see what Kenneth White calls "the primal gesture."

Calanais' configuration was almost certainly built in phases, and has been described as a "Celtic Cross" measuring 400 feet from north to south, and 155 feet from east to west. A height-gradated avenue of 19 stones heads the cross, and a row of 5 runs south. Other lines radiate roughly east (5 stones) and west (4 stones). A cramped inner circle is comprised of 13 tall stones and a towering (15'9") central monolith that is aligned almost perfectly N-S. The geometry of Calanais is almost identical to that of Kilmartin's Temple Wood, and the stone shapes are similar to those chosen for circles in Argyll as well as in Orkney.

The central monolith watches over a compact tomb built later than the circle construction, in which cremated remains were found. A position at the north end of the avenue of standing stones was probably used for lunar observations. The avenues themselves indicate the southerly extreme moonset. The axis of symmetry in the inner ring points east.

Stones forming the north avenue are highest at each end and stones on the west side of the avenue are consistently smaller than those on the east. These details are similar to monuments in the north of Ireland. Calanais was built and added to from around 3000 BCE to 1500 BCE and bears a stronger resemblance to Orcadian design than to local Hebridean style.

Sometime around 1500-1000 BCE the monument fell into disuse and suffered minor despoiling by Bronze Age farmers. During that same period, however, those farmers seem to have added large kerb stones to the cairn's north side, replacing a walling of smaller stones. Artifacts found by archaeologists reveal that the monument users had trade contact with people on mainland Scotland and in Ireland.

Calanais, set on the north-south ridge, is oriented to equinox sunrises, has an alignment to the Pleiades, and is well situated for lunar observations – as Stonehenge is oriented and well located for solar observations. The Western and Northern

Isles are so far north that progressive lunar and solar movements cover a wide arc of the horizon and – that horizon having prominent, fixed features – it is easy to plot movements against it.

Placed in megalithic building sequence, Calanais comes slightly after Stenness in Orkney, and before Stonehenge. The monument draws the observer in, inviting touch, consideration, unwillingness to just glance around, snap a photo, and leave. Impressive monuments like Calanais are inspiring, but the number of tourists tramping through year in and year out can't help but dilute their atmosphere. In contrast are some of the less trafficked circles; there are several in the Calanais neighbourhood.

Cnoc Ceann a' Gharraidh (Hillock at the End of the Wall)
    5/8 miles ESE of Calanais. (NB 222 326)
    An easy walk 600 yards SW of the A858.
    Only 100 yards from Loch Roag.

An elliptical circle of 5 remaining stones between 6.5 and 10 feet tall, the tallest at the NE. The circle is 71' N-S by 62'. There is a dispersed cairn at the centre. Remains were found of the circle's original timber construction.

Cnoc Fillibhir Bheag (Little Fillibhir Hillock)
¾ miles ESE of Calanais, close to the main circle. (NB 225 325) Walk ¼ mile west of the A858; easy access.

An egg-shaped or flattened circle of 8 tall standing and 5 fallen stones. 4 even taller stones form an oval cove in the inner area. The tallest is 7', on the NNW of the longer axis. There is no cairn in this circle, which seems to have lunar orientations.

Ceann Hulavaig (Head of Hula Bay)
2 miles SSE of Calanais. (NB 230 304) Take the B8011 from Garynahine toward Uig. About a mile along, you'll see the

tops of the stones on rising ground to the right, a short walk from the road.

A 43'7" SSE-NNW by 31' elliptical circle of (out of a possible 13) 5 stones. The stones range from 6 to 9 feet high, the tallest at the SSE end of the long axis. There is a poorly drained hollow in the centre in which cairn stones remain. The largest cairn stone is set on edge, lying on the main axis of the circle's ellipse. This major axis points toward the *Calanais circle* and is an approximate indication of summer solstice sunset. There are also lunar alignments for the rising of June's full moon at the southern extreme of the major lunar standstill.

Every 18.61 years, for a few nights, the moon rises so close to due south that its path across the sky is less than 2' above the horizon. At Calanais this moon path rises out of the Pairc Hills (Cailleach na Mointeach – The Sleeping Woman), skims that ranges of hills, and sets into the Clisham Hills. In all the Calanais circles, the long axes are directed to a solar or lunar extreme. The most recent major lunar event at Calanais occurred in 2006.

An interesting side trip from Calanais is a drive up to the *Butt of Lewis*, to the lighthouse there. Take the A858 north from Calanais to the A857, stopping at the *Dun Carloway Broch*, (NB 190 412) the *Clach na Tursa* standing stone, the *Arnol Blackhouses*, the massive *Clach na Trushal* standing stone, (NB 375 538) and the *Steinacleit Cairn and Circle* on your way.

To proceed from Ness to North Uist, head back south on the A857, through Stornoway and onto the A859 to the south end of Harris.[11] (There are some magnificent sand beaches on the west coast of Harris.) The ferry to North Uist is at Leverburgh, and goes to Berneray; or, there is a ferry from Skye to Lochmaddy, North Uist.

Lochmaddy is the chief port of North Uist and the location of services such as banking, post

---

[11] **Harris Tweed** is the traditional famed fabric made in the Western Isles, hand-woven by islanders, of Scottish wool. You may notice weaving sheds beside many crofthouse, as much of this work is done at home. The tweed industry has its ups and downs, but a Harris Tweed coat lasts forever.

office, hotel, hostel, and Tourist Office.[12] North Uist is low-lying, absolutely pot-holed with lochans; there are exquisite white sand beaches on the west coast.

Neolithic Sites on North Uist

Caranais Stone Circle (Charity/Alms Circle)
- The main road runs straight through this circle, but it is in such a ruinous state that it is not easily spotted.
- *Date*: Neolithic
- *Configuration*: An oval ring of 41.5 metres by 39 metres, made up of 6 remaining stones, the highest of which stands about a metre. Many of the stones are leaning badly and becoming buried in the peat.

Barpa Langais Chambered Cairn

---

[12] **Sabbath observances** are most strict in Lewis and Harris. Visitors should be aware that businesses and services do not operate on Sundays, so plan accordingly.

- Just east of the Langais road, on the slope of Ben Langais, 5 miles north of Lochmaddy. (NF 838 657)
- *Date*: Neolithic
- *Configuration*: 25 metres in diameter, over 4 metres high. A lintelled passage grave with its entrance on the east side. The intact polygonal chamber has 7 uprights with walling between; the lintels are huge!
- *Alignments*: East-facing entrance.
- *Artifacts*: Cremated bone, pottery, and flint objects were found in the chamber.
- *Condition*: Not bad.

Pobull Fhinn (White/Holy People, or Finn's People)

- Off the A867 5 miles WSW of Lochmaddy, at Langais. (NF 844 650) A half-mile SE of Barpa Langais Cairn. Down a farm track, then walk 250 yards; easy access.
- *Configuration*: An embanked circle with portalled entrances at either end of its long

axis. An ellipse of 37.8 metres by 28 metres. The tallest stone is 1.8 metres; there are 30 stones (some fallen) out of the original 48.
- *Alignments*: built on a south-facing slope of Ben Langais.
- *Condition*: Recognizable.

Marrogh Chambered Cairn (NF 833 696)
- *Configuration*: 24 metres in diameter, 4 metres high, on moorland. An eastern entrance between 2 portal stones.
- The passage is now filled with stone but the passage roof lintels are still intact, unlike those of the circular chamber. The chamber is constructed of massive uprights with walling between and is 3 metres in diameter. There is an outlying standing stone 100 metres SW of the cairn.

Loch a' Phobuill Stone Circle (Loch of the People) (NF 829 630)

- 6.5 miles SW of Lochmaddy and a mile SE of Clachan. Off the B894. A 550 yard walk.
- *Date*: Neolithic
- *Configuration*: 16 stones remain of a possible 50 in the 130' (SE-NW) by 115' ellipse. There is a large gap in the eastern quadrant of the circle, and 2 slabs on edge just inside the circle at ENE and SE, both arranged SE-NW. The ring is cut into the hillside to make a platform.
- *Alignments*: Possibly aligned to the Unival Chambered Cairn 3 miles to the NW; the midsummer sun would set behind that cairn.
- *Type of Stone*: Granite.
- *Condition*: Ruined

Unival Chambered Cairn

- Off the A865, 1.5 miles north of Claddach Illeray, south of Unival. (NF 800 668)
- *Configuration*: A square cairn. Upright stones line the entrance, passage, and cham-

ber walls; the tallest stone is that at the passage entrance.

- *Artifacts*: A cist was found containing burnt bone fragments. A mix of bone and pottery fragments were scattered around the chamber's walls.

Additional Sites on North Uist:[13]

- *Dun an Sticar Broch* (NF 898 778) contains remains of a medieval house.
- *Dun Torcuill Broch* (NF 888 737) Located on a crannog.
- *Na Fir Bhreige Standing Stones*
- *Clettraval Cairn & Standing Stones*

Leaving the Western Isles, again there are route options: air flight from Stornoway; the Stornoway ferry to Ullapool on the mainland – and

---

[13] On some of the lochs, you'll see small natural or artificial islands with large piles of stones or ruined walls on them. These are the remains of *crannogs*, a form of fortified settlement also seen in some other parts of Scotland. Each such island has a path of stones leading to it just under the surface of the water. One good example of a crannog on North Uist is dun Torcuill, just off the A865 north of Lochmaddy.

road travel from Ullapool to Inverness (the A835 is the main route); or returning on the ferry to Skye from Tarbert, Harris, or from Lochmaddy, North Uist. On Skye, travel down the A87 to the Skye Bridge, and over to Kyle, continuing on the A87 to the A887, to Invermoriston, to Drumnadrochit and turn left onto the A831 to visit Corrimony Cairn.

Inverness-shire

Inverness is a thriving area, tourism only one of its strengths. Though touted as the capital of the Highlands, Inverness is actually "East Coast," this difference evidenced in the shire's terrain, weather, and culture.

It is an attractive area in its own right, rich in green pastures, lovely corners such as **Glen Affric**, trees and farms, busy communities. Inverness, now a city, is full of shops, restaurants, and enterprise, and is a transportation hub for planes, trains, and buses. Accommodation of all sorts abounds in the region. **Loch Ness** is a visitor magnet, as is the **Moray Firth**. There are boat tours; castles such as the ruined **Urquhart** and well-furnished **Cawdor**; two *"monster" museums*; the delights of **Eden Court Theatre**; festivals and music; and a number of Neolithic and Bronze Age sites dotted around the countryside.

Corrimony Cairn

At Glen Urquhart, 8.5 miles west of Drumnadrochit (Loch Ness) off the A831, on the left. (NH 383 303) Roadside access, very easy.

Corrimony, beside a rural lane, is an attractive monument, encompassable in size but large enough to command attention. The monument is set with fairly open views across the fields to near and distant hills. There are trees lining the rural lane, and a burn runs close to the stones.

The site, which is remarkably well preserved, comprises a ring of standing stones, surrounding a substantial cairn. This is not a true circle, but neither does it conform to any of the regular types, consequently is designated an "irregular" ring some 70' in diameter. There are 11 stones in the ring, 4 of which are modern additions or re-established originals. 2 stones to the west of the entrance are in fact composite structures.

The commanding cairn, surrounded by the irregular ring, is established on an ovoid platform of about 61' NE-SW by 56', and measure 50' by 45' along the same axes. A Clava-type passage-grave, it has a neatly circular burial chamber at its heart. This is slightly over 12' in diameter and although it is now unroofed, is estimated to have been 8' in height. The floor of the low passage is constructed from flat flagstones or river-worn rock and the chamber itself is floored with packed yellow sand and flagstones. Some charcoal was found here during an excavation in 1952, apparently sufficient to suggest a "crouched inhumation." A bone pin was also found in the passageway.

On top of the cairn, which, as mentioned above, is now open to the elements, is a single large slab – possibly the original capstone of the chamber, – which bears many cup-marks.

Balnuaran of Clava

From Corrimony, backtrack to Drumnadrochit and continue toward Inverness on the A887. Follow signs for the A9 to Perth, then exit onto the B9006, past the Culloden Monument, and follow road-signs to the "Clava Cairns," about 1.5 miles SE of the Culloden monument.[14] Very easy access. (NH 757 444)

One of the things that make Balnuaran of Clava special is its trees. Inverness-shire does have wonderful trees. Those at Balnuaran are mostly beeches. The rhythm of their cycles, and their rich colour and flickering leaves, counterpoint the stillness of the stones. Like trees in any cemetery, Clava's trees are consoling; tactfully cheerful.

Clava – or more properly, Balnuaran of Clava – since Clava is a generic term referring to the monument style – consists of 2 chambered cairns separated by a ring cairn, each surrounded by

---

[14] On your way to Balnuaran of Clava, you'll pass the ***Culloden Battlefield***, well worth a visit, though not cheery to contemplate. Culloden was Bonnie Prince Charlie's final stand, after which he cut and ran, leaving the clans to a brutal aftermath in 1746.

a stone circle. Balnuaran is part of a linear cemetery extending along the valley (some others in this line are mentioned in "Additional Sites"). Most of the ring cairns at these sites probably pre-date their mound cairns, constructed around 2000 BCE. The Clava cairns all face southwest, their passages aligned toward midwinter sunset.

Despite its size and duration of use, Balnuaran apparently was used for only a few burials. The 2 chambered cairns, though far apart, appear to have been constructed as a unit, their entrances on a line with one another. The NE cairn originally was roofed with a dome, though is open now. The standing stones of the circles are size-gradated with the tallest in the SW quadrant. This too is typical of monuments in the region. Some of the circle stones and cairn stones are carved with cupmarks. Among circles in the Inverness area, 96% of them contain cairns or internal burials, a much higher percentage than among circles in other regions. Where stones have cup-markings, or where stones are height-gradated, it is likely that the circles contain burials and have lunar alignments.

In marked contrast with compact Corrimony, Balnuaran occurs on a grand scale. The site has a gracious ambiance, sitting as it does in a wooded hollow surrounded by fertile grazing. I have visited Balnuaran at least half a dozen times, and whatever the season and weather, it is a place that invites contemplation.

One of the first things noticed about this site is the size of the megaliths – huge. The 3 cairns lie – the centre cairn offset – along a NE-SW line approximately 350' long. West of the central (ring) cairn is a small, low kerbed circle, off on its own. This was built 1000
years after the main cairns, making it about 3000 years old. One of its stones is cup, and cup-and-ring, marked.

The NE cairn is surrounded by an elliptical ring, its major axis running NE-SW – the same orientation as the cairns – of 114' by 104'. The circle consists of 11 stones, though there may once have been 12. The west stone is 9' tall. The cairn inside is 55' in diameter and 10' tall, standing on an upraised base. The passage, running SW, is 20' long, leading to an inner chamber 148" in diameter – identical to that of Corrimony. Bones were found in this chamber during an 1854 excavation.

There are cup marks on a north-facing kerbstone looking out over the stump of an outer-circle stone. There are also cup-marks on one of the slabs at the western end of the chamber passage, which is aligned to midwinter sunset.

Moving to the central ring cairn, the circle surrounding it is a true circle of 103'. Again the tallest stone is to the west, actually WSW, and stands at 7.5' high. There are 3 causeways radiating from the cairn toward the surrounding circle. These run like spokes from the cairn mound to the megaliths. They are low mounds, not always easily discerned, but radiate in easterly, southeasterly, and west-northwesterly directions. The cairn itself is ovoid, 60' by 52'. Cremated bone deposits were uncovered in this tomb. There are also cup-marks on this cairn, to the east and southeast.

The final, SW, cairn is surrounded by a circle of 11 stones, all of local sandstone. Several had collapsed and were re-erected circa 1876. The cairn within has a NE-SW orientation and is some 52' across. Vases were reported to have been found in the digs of 1828-29, containing fragments of cremated bone. We noticed cup-marks inside the cairn's passage and on the west stone of the outer circle.

As well as height gradations in all the configurations, there are colour arrangements of the stones, using red/pink and grey to make patterns.

Additional Sites

Culdoich Stone Circle (also called Miltown of Clava)

- Three-quarters mile SW of Balnuaran of Clava, a quarter-mile west of Ballagan farm, ESE of Inverness. (NH 751 438)

- *Configuration*: A 59' ring-cairn with gradated kerb stones to the SW. The southern arc of the ring has been destroyed by quarrying. A huge (12' high by 8' wide) cup-marked standing stone is 27' SW of the ring cairn.
- *Alignments*: The outlier may be oriented to the minor moonset.
- *Artifacts*: Under the clay-floored open space within the cairn, charcoal and the cremated bones of two people were found.
- *Condition*: Recognizable.

Daviot

- 2¾ miles SW of Balnuaran of Clava, 4½ miles SE of Inverness, off the B851. (NH 727 411) A walk of 250 yards through trees. Easy access.
- *Configuration*: A Clava-style ring cairn, elliptical (50'2" E-W by 47'7") with a central space 18' across. The cairn has a gradated kerbing, somewhat ruined. The large

block at the SW faces a 9'6" tall pillar that is one of the only remaining stones of the 90' surrounding circle.
- *Artifacts*: A cist was found containing a skull and other burial remains.
- *Condition*: Recognizable.

Druidtemple
- 4¼ miles WSW of Balnuaran of Clava, 2¼ miles south of Inverness, behind Druidtemple Farm. (NH 685 420) Take the B861 from Inverness to Balloan and turn east ¾ miles to Hilton, then SE 1 mile to the west lane to the farm. Easy access.
- *Configuration*: Clava-style passage-grave on a ridge, 5 stones remain of the 15-stone, 74'4" ring, much ruined. Inside is an elliptical kerbed cairn, 43'6" SSE-NNW by 38', with a ruined passage and chamber. The chamber originally was floored with quartz pebbles.

- *Alignments*: The tallest stone (9'6") at the west of the cairn entrance lines up with midwinter sunset. The cairn passage, unusually, orients south-north.
- *Artifacts*: In the Bronze Age someone stashed an intricately decorated gold torc or funicular rod here. Two cists were also found, both empty.
- *Condition*: Recognizable.

Gask

- Just east of the B861, a quarter-mile north of Hilton, 3¼ miles SW of Daviot. (NH 679 358) Easy access
- *Configuration*: A large Clava-type ring cairn built in several stages above the River Nairn. 3 remaining stones (the tallest is 11'11", in the SSW) in the 119' gradated ring around a ruined cairn. The kerb stones, also gradated, surround an 82'10" cairn irregularly placed inside the circle. One of the fallen circle stones (NE) has 3 cup-marks.

- *Condition*: Recognizable.

Tordarroch
- 4.5 miles SW of Daviot, 7.5 miles south of Inverness, on the east side of the lane from Farr to Tordarroch, an easy 200-yard walk. (NH679 334)
- *Configuration*: A large Clava-style ring cairn surrounded by a 113' circle with 7 out of the 11 stones still standing, gradated to the SSW. The irregular-shaped inner cairn is in poor condition, but one of the kerb stones in the SSW has over 30 cup-marks.
- *Alignments*: The tallest stone in the circle (over 9' high) is aligned with the cup-marked kerb slab and with the major southern moonset.
- *Condition*: Recognizable.

Aviemore Stone Circle
- Just east of the A9, 4.5 miles SW of Boat of Garten, 11.5 miles NE of Kingussie, in a

housing estate at the north end of Aviemore.
Easy to see. (NH 896 134)
- *Configuration*: A Clava-style ring cairn; 5 stones remain of at least 7 in a 76' circle. The tallest (almost 5') is in the SW of the height-gradated ring. The inside cairn kerb is height-gradated too. There is little left of the cairn and central space, which is lined by 3-4 remaining slabs.
- *Condition*: Recognizable.

Delfour
- 4 miles SW of Aviemore, 2 miles NNE of Kincraig, off the A9 and a quarter-mile NW down a lane of trees to a SW turn at Easter Delfour. (NH 844 085) Easy access alongside a track.
- *Configuration*: A 60' ring cairn with SW-gradated kerbing around a central space 28' across, interrupted at the SW. The surrounding stone circle has only 1 stone, which may instead be an outlier, 9.5' high.

- *Alignments:* The tall pillar orients to mid-winter sunset.
- *Condition*: Recognizable.

Bruiach Stone Circle

- A half-mile SE of Culburnie ring cairn, 3.5 miles SW of Beauly, at the lane junction from Aultfearn to Culburnie. (NH 499 414) Walk 200 yards SW. Easy access.
- *Configuration*: A stone circle 73' in diameter, of fairly low stones, containing a ring cairn 47' across. Of the kerb stones surrounding the cairn, 2 are cup-marked (S & NW stones). The cairn and circle may have been built at different times.
- *Condition*: Recognizable.

Culburnie Stone Circle

- A half-mile NW of the Bruiach ring, 3.5 miles SW of Beauly. (NH 491 418) An easy walk west from a house a quarter-mile north of the minor road.

- *Configuration*: 8 stones of the original 9 form a 70' height-gradated ring. The stones range from about 3' (NNE) to 8' (SSW) high. The cairn has been wrecked and is now only 5' high, kerbed with large blocks and having a 17' wide central space. Cup-marks may be noted on several stones.
- *Type of Stone*: The tallest circle stone is mica schist.
- *Condition*: Recognizable.

Turning from the bustle of Inverness, go north up the A9 past the fertile Black Isle, over the Dornoch Firth, past **Dunrobin Castle**, following the coast road as it rises and drops and, in some places, tightly twists and turns. Up past Helmsdale, once teeming with herring boats, past Neil Gunn's Dunbeath, the cold North Sea always asserting its presence – the inland straths and hills now largely empty – until reaching the village with the unlikely name of Latheron.[15]

---

[15] For those wanting sidetrips to sites in **Sutherland**:

Caithness

Most tourists never venture to Caithness, in the far north of the Scottish mainland, but it is an area rich in antiquities, an evocative landscape and history, a place of hardy people with close links to Orkney.

The coasts of Caithness include everything from sandy beaches, fantastical cliffs and rock formations, to the sites of world surfing championships.[16] Both the coasts and the inland lochs,

---

1. *Achany Stone Circle* -- near Lairg. (NC 560 029) Oval ring.
2. *Shin River Circle* -- near Lairg. (NC 582 049) 2 ruinous rings.
3. *Abercross Stone Circle* -- near Golspie. (NH 770 991) Ring and cist.
4. *Cnoc an Laith-Bhaid* -- near Braegrudie (NC 728 102) Radially-set rings.
5. *Learable Hills Cairns & Circles* -- Helmsdale area. (NC 895 241) Multiple rows, standing stones, 2 circles, cairn.

Brochs:
- *Kilphedir* -- (NC 995 189) Hilltop, but circle also.
- *Dun Dornaigil* -- (NC 457 450) Well preserved.
- *Cairn Liath* -- near Golspie. (NC 870 013).

[16] Two spectacular coastal spots to visit are **Duncansby Head** with its nesting colonies of kittiwakes, fulmars, razorbills, guillemots, and puffins crowding the red sandstone cliffs and

peatlands, and marshes attract large numbers of a variety of birds at different times of year; and the terrain itself is home to a range of plant life, some of which is rare and particular to that ecosystem.

There is richer pasture here than in the Highlands and Islands, yet in Caithness you really *feel* how far north you are. It is not just the very long summer days and very short winter ones, or the reality of "land's end" at John O'Groats; it is something in the landscape itself that humbles the visitor – a gift of perspective.

Wick is the region's capital, though Thurso is in some ways the busier town. The area has bus and train transport, but a car may be needed to visit the Neolithic sites. Accommodation is best sought in Wick or Thurso, though there are B&Bs in smaller villages, and sometimes hotels also. Thurso has several hostels. As well as the older antiquities, Caithness has fine brochs and duns, and dramati-

---

seastacks; and **Noss Head** with its cliffs and coastal features, its breeding seabird colonies, lighthouse, and the ancient ruined castle of Girnigoe. Both headlands are north of Wick.

cally situated castle ruins such as *Forse*, *Oldwick*, *Bucholie*, and *Girnigoe*, worth exploring.

Taking the A9 north from Inverness, traffic thins out once you pass the Dornoch Firth. This, and the fact that the North's antiquities are often unmarked by sign or visitor centre, adds a feeling of privacy and discovery even in peak season.

Guidebest Stone Circle

300 yards off the track between Jamestown and Den Moss, (ND 181 351).

This site requires some of that appetite for discovery. The circle sits in a hollow beside a burn, down a long slope of fenced pasture and small stands of trees.

The circle is generous in diameter, though the stones themselves are not huge. Guidebest seems peaceful, holding its own amid farms, cattle, sheep, and benign neglect.

When this circle was in pristine shape, it constituted one of the largest diameter circles in

Scotland, some 188' across. Unfortunately, only 8 of the conjectured 13 open-spaced stones remain, and one of these has fallen. The remnant extends in a broad arc running south through west to north, and nothing is to be seen of the eastern arc. The largest surviving stone, a little less than 5' tall, marks the western limit of the arc. Two small cairns, one to the NE and the other to the south, lie just beyond the boundary of the ring.

Achavanich or Achinloch

From Guidebest, return to Latheron and the road to Thurso, turning off 6 miles along, onto a single-track leading to Loch Stemster. The site is just SW of the loch, beside the road; easy access. (ND 188 417).

Achavanich was built as a "horseshoe" configuration, beautifully constructed and still in good condition. There are 34 stones on the site, arranged radially, the horseshoe open to the SSE. The stones are of local sandstone and are typically "playing-card" in shape, and not tall. A cist is apparent at the northern curve of the structure, but there is no record of what, if anything, it once contained. The structure does appear to be aligned on the major southern moonrise; the opening at 160°.

A little distance to the SE are the prominent remains of a chambered cairn. Though badly damaged, the underlying structure is recognizable and the central chamber can be discerned. The entrance to the tomb appears to have been from the east.

The Grey Cairns of Camster

5 miles north of Lybster; signposted; easy access. (ND 260 442)

Camster did not live up to expectations. I'd always imagined the tomb stretched out on a bleak northern moor, hostile, windswept, rain-lashed, and really not very alluring. But it is not anything like that! The stone structures are a warm grey and occupy an attractive situation just a few yards from the road. Sensitively restored, and connected to the road by an unobtrusive boardwalk over the heather and bog, this site is one of the best examples I've seen of balanced preservation and presentation.

      The main structure, defined as a long horned cairn, has been reconstructed and maintained. The cairn, in shape not dissimilar to an elongated mermaid's purse, runs NE-SW, and contains two chambered passage cells. The more northerly of the two – both are accessed from the west – appears to be the older original structure consisting of a polygonal chamber. Its neighbour is of a tripartite construction, simpler but basically not dissimilar to the forms of Maes Howe or Newgrange. Both of these Camster chambers began as individual round cairns, which later were joined by stacking tons of stone to create the long cairn. The horns extending from the northern and southern corners of the structure contain platforms and define a space at either end suggesting that on appropriate dates these areas may have been used in ritual.

Between the road and the long cairn is ***Camster Round***. This cairn is largely intact; most of the internal structure in passage and chamber has survived the millennia. Keep in mind that these cairns were built before the Pyramids. Like the southern chamber in Camster Long, this chamber is tripartite in construction, and the passage (7 yards long) faces east.

We saw a few people wandering the site during our visit, but we were the only ones who seemed inclined to actually enter the cairns. Entry is through low narrow passages where it helps if your build is fairly slim. Not places for the claustrophobic. In the tripartite passages, as you squeeze along in the dark, you first reach an antechamber, then the spaciousness of the pillared chamber itself, which is dimly lit by a translucent panel letting in natural light. This is great because the stonework is wonderful to see!

The Hill O' Many Stanes or Mid-Clyth Stone Rows

Signposted off the A9 south of Wick. (ND 295 384) Easy access.

This is an unusual configuration for those of us living farther south: stone rows. You park, climb a short rise, and encounter the startlement of fan-shaped rows. Many stanes indeed – hundreds – though not as many as originally; and such wee stones they are, a tribe of dwarfs. The impact is bewildering. You open your mouth and are not quite sure what to say.

This configuration seems particular to the north of Scotland – over 20 such sites have been found in Caithness and Sutherland. More doubtless are still hidden under the peat. Similar settings, using taller stones, are found in Brittany.

This site dates from the Bronze Age. Professor Thom stated that the rows, containing about 200 stones, are arranged in a geometrical pattern, fanning out as they run from north to south. Thom suggests that the rows could have been used as a complex lunar observatory, perhaps for calculating the extreme positions of the moon in her 18.6-year cycle. Some stone rows – although not fan-shaped – are known to be associated with burials.

Garrywhin or Cairn of Get

On a track off the A9, south of Wick. (ND 313 411) Fair but not difficult walk.

The final stop in this cluster of sites involves a partially boardwalked path leading to the cairn, but the site does not seem much trafficked. Garrywhin is a short horned cairn, elliptical in shape, with a polygonal chamber and small antechamber, all of it roofless now, which offers an interesting bird's-eye view of the interior. The internal chamber is a simple
construction using vertical slabs to form the walls, but vertical slabs are also used to define an antechamber between passage and tomb, which more typically is seen in sophisticated later-built struc-

tures. Unlike the Camster cairns, this cairn is entered from the SSW.

Garrywhin is not a big imposing monument, but beautifully laid out and harmonious with its setting, a place of wildflowers, birds, views, and the sound of the wind over the moor.

Additional sites
Cnoc Freiceadain Cairn (Hillock of the Sentinel)
- Several miles east of Reay, just north of Shebster. (ND 013 654) Signposted.
- *Configuration*: Two long horned cairns on the crest of a hill with wonderful views over Caithness and out to Orkney. The tombs are covered in turf and have not been excavated.

Na Tri Shean (possibly The Three Amulets or Three Ancients)
- Oriented SE-NW and is about 70 metres long and 18-23 metres wide.

- The cairn rises at either end into circular mounds with what may be disturbed lintel stones projecting from the cairn.

Cnoc Freiceadain

- The second cairn, at right angles from the first, is about 67 metres by 17 metres, with a raised round cairn at the SW end. Slabs protrude from this mound as well.

Ousdale Broch (ND 072 188)

- Best preserved broch in Caithness.

Yarrows Broch (ND 308 435)

- Set on a promontory.

There are two ferry routes to Orkney from Caithness: the passenger ferry from John O'Groats to South Ronaldsay; and the car ferry from Scrabster (by Thurso)[17] to Stromness, on Orkney main-

---

[17] In Thurso Museum, at the library, are several very fine sculptured stones dating from the Pictish period. The **Ulbster Stone** in particular is amazing work with more symbols carved on it than any other known stone of its type.

land. Either crossing can be especially memorable if the wind is up.

John O'Groats is at the end of the A99 north of Wick; and Scrabster is at the end of the A9, just beyond Thurso.

Orkney

When in Orkney I sometimes have to remind myself of the proximity of mainland Scotland; Orkney seems a world unto itself and, indeed, is said to be such by Orcadians. By the end of 2000 I'd made four trips to Orkney; each trip left a taste for more. Orkney puzzles that way – undramatic in much of its scenery, foul in much of its weather, but something about the place gets under the skin and there's an itch to return.

A wonderful place to stay is the village of ***Stromness*** with its narrow flagstone streets, and outlooks to the sea and the Isle of Hoy; Stromness has much to recommend it, including a very satisfying bookstore.

Kirkwall is Orkney's main town and boasts a leading jewellery centre and a whisky distillery, as well as the magnificent ***St. Magnus Cathedral***, the wicked Earl's ruined palace, and a fascinating museum.

There are a variety of accommodation options in Orkney, though outside Kirkwall and Stromness visitors mainly rely on B&Bs and hostels. Bus and ferry services are plentiful, routes that take you to the doorsteps of mainland Orkney's premier Neolithic sites.

Despite how far north it is, there is much farming in Orkney[18] – cattle and sheep, cultivated fields, stone barns, tractors cruising the long low hills. But like other Scottish islands, Orkney also looks to the sea. The human component is a mix of Norse, Celt, and

more recent southern incomers. Events such as World War II and the discovery of North Sea oil had a profound effect on Orcadian life.

The Neolithic monuments of Orkney are a considerable tourist draw. As a farmer on the island once said to me, "You can't walk out your door

---

[18] Souterrains are underground stone passages with slabbed roofs, dating to the Iron Age. Some have chambers or compartments within them, and may have been used for storage and/or ritual purposes. Two good examples of souterrains are found on Orkney: The **Grain Souterrain** with its oval chamber; and the **Rennibister Souterrain** whose chamber has alcoves and pillars.

without falling into some tomb." Orkney abounds in chambered cairns, and though there are not many stone circles here, the ones they have are BIG.

Orkney in Neolithic times was a centre of cultural trade and power. It probably was climate change, more than anything else, that was responsible for that centrality's decline.

The Stones of Stenness

> 5 miles northeast of Stromness, off the A965 to Kirkwall. (HY 306 125) Easy access.

No one has won the Turner Prize – the annual Arts awards – with a work even fractionally as dramatic as the Stones of Stenness. The monument is at once ancient, modern, minimalist, with an uncluttered and unfussy purity of form. Even as they are, a much reduced assemblage from the original 10 or 12 stones, these megaliths constitute a magnificent group.

The Stones of Stenness is a henge monument, once deeply ditched and banked on its perimeter. The entrance is north of a central stone hearth used for cremations; excavations have shown that a timber post once stood in the centre. A low table-like structure, off from the centre, was fabricated in 1906. The four remaining stones of the circle are the tallest group I've seen in Scotland – stirringly, starkly tall.

It is estimated that this group was raised between 3000 and 2500 BCE – probably closer to the earlier date. The ring, which must have taken roughly 5,000 man-days to complete, is elliptical, measuring about 104' by 98', and oriented 20° to the east of south. A soaring outlier, called the Watch Stone, stands well to the south, at the end of someone's driveway.

Located so close to the Stenness monument that one cannot be disassociated from the other, is the **Barnhouse** settlement, which may have housed the specialists of megalithic building. The settlement remains beguile with their tidy scale, built-in flagstone furniture, loch-side location, and proximity to the big monuments. Three perfect enclosures – dwellings or ceremonial halls – stripped to their blueprints, open to the imagination.

The Ring Of Brogar (or Brodgar)
1 mile southwest from Stenness, and within view of it. (HY 294 133) Easy access.

Going up the road from Stenness to Brogar, you pass a collection of farm buildings called Brodgar Cottage, on your left. These buildings exemplify the traditional style of building in these islands: gravity the concrete of a clipped austerity that after centuries continues to press roof timbers firmly down onto still true walls.

Passing these buildings, the eye is drawn next to the Comet Stone, a satellite of the principle ring. Raised on a platform with its own companion stones, the Comet Stone lies in a line between Brogar, Stenness, Barnhouse, and Maes Howe.

The Ring of Brogar is so big – 334.7' across – that focus is drawn more to its perimeter than to what it may enclose. Brogar is a true circle, and considered the best of its type in the world. There used to be 60 stones surrounded by a deep ditch cut into solid bedrock. Imagine the work this demanded! 36 stones remain, the western stone being the tallest at 15'. Causeways bridge the ditch in the northwest and southeast. The ring was built between 3000 and 2000 BCE, after the construction of Stenness and Maes Howe.

The setting of this Orkney grouping seems similar to that at Calanais, on the Isle of Lewis. There is water on several sides; distant hills; a concentration of major and satellite monuments; the two sites were erected during the same era, and in a context of island location and climate.

Brogar's ring seems complete even with its missing and fallen stones. The individual stones exude character – perhaps an odd thing to say about stone, but their forms and textures do confer a sense of personality. One of the ring stones at Brodgar was struck by a bolt of lightning in recent years, a cleaved section of it lies, massively, where it fell.

The most northerly and southerly stones stand very true to north and south; the easternmost and westernmost stones are offset slightly to the north of the magnetic cardinals.[19] There are several outlying cairns associated with this ring, and two pairs of these, lying close to the ditch, form sight-lines to the NE (or SW) and to the NW (or SE). These are significant as regards the rising and setting points of the midsummer and midwinter sun. It has been suggested that these mounds could have also played a role in lunar observation. There are other outlying mounds, and a cairn to the SW of the

---

[19] If you continue on the B9056 beyond the Ring of Brogar for several miles, you'll reach the best-preserved Neolithic village in Northern Europe: **Skara Brae**. It was occupied from around 3100 BCE to 2450 BCE, then gradually buried in sand, and not discovered until a storm exposed it in 1850. The preservation is remarkable – daily life is revealed in the flagstone hearth, beds, dressers, and shelves of these low stone houses, now roofless, that were connected to one another by low stone passages. The Skara Brae visitor centre displays artifacts and a video presentation; you pay to view the site. Open all year.

ring. Several of these have been excavated, in one case revealing a cremation urn.

Maes Howe

9 miles west of Kirkwall, off the A965. (HY 318 128) Entrance fee and restricted hours of access.

Maes Howe doesn't look like much from the outside. It is visible from the road, a grassy mound in a field. A path leads to it from the visitor centre. It is upon entering the cairn that the place becomes astonishing.

A guide leads small groups down a stone-lined 53' passage into the heart of the tomb. The passage is oriented to winter solstice sunset. After the lecture in the inner chamber, the guide switches off the electric lights and, with a flashlight, demonstrates how the solstice light beams down the long passage to illumine the rear chamber. It calls to mind a similar arrangement at Newgrange, in

Ireland, the oldest known human construction on earth.

Maes Howe is considered the finest chambered tomb in the UK. The 115' mound dates to circa 3000 BCE and contains a 16' chamber meticulously constructed from sandstone slabs. The corbelled barrel-vault ceiling is 15' high. Three raised side-cells elaborate a design that is a marvel of aesthetics, engineering, and stone-craft. The heavy entrance stone swings easily, positioned to be sealed from inside the passage, yet still allowing the shaft of light to enter above.

An unusual feature of the chamber is the Viking graffiti; 24 cocky runes inscribed on the walls during a 12th century break-in. Some things never change.

The guide told us that there is a 15-year waiting list of people wanting to be inside Maes Howe during midwinter sunset – and of course no promise that the usual clouds won't obscure those crucial moments of light. Nostalgia for the good old Neolithic days when Orkney was sunnier, is understandable.

Additional Sites

There are two main cairn types on Orkney: The Orkney-Cromarty-Hebridean type in which the chambers are divided into compartments by upright slabs; and the Maes Howe type in which the passage leads to a chamber with side-cells.

Cuween Hill Chambered Cairn
- Off the A965, 7 miles NW of Kirkwall, a half-mile south of Finstown, on the NE side of a hill. (HY 364 128)
- A rectangular chamber with a small cell on each side (the west one is divided in two) inside a 16' diameter cairn. The chamber is entered on the east side. The remains of 8 inhumation burials and the skulls of 14 dogs were found inside.

The dogs probably had totem association with that area's people.

Dwarfie Stane
- Off the B9047 at the north end of the Isle of Hoy. (HY 243 004)
- This cairn is a tremendous block of red sandstone, 8.5 metres by 4.5 metres; a passage and 2 cells were cut into its west side. The cells are divided by a kerb; one cell has a low step or pillow in it. There is a blocking stone at the entrance. A unique monument.

Unstan Cairn
- Off the A965, 3 miles NE of Stromness. (HY 283 118)
- An Orkney-style cairn built of concentric rings of walling, into a circular mound on a promontory on the Loch of Stenness. Excavation turned up pottery sherds,

arrowheads, flint, inhumation burials, and animal and bird bones.

Blackhammer Cairn
- On the B9065, Isle of Rousay. (HY 415 276)
- Its rectangular central chamber is divided into 7 compartments originally entered from the south. There is now a concrete entrance hatch. The cairn contained 2 inhumation burials.

Knowe of Yarso – Isle of Rousay (HY 405 280)
- A rectangular, compartmented chamber within a cairn 15m by 8m, and 1.8 metres high. At least 29 burials were found here; also flint and bone objects, pottery sherds, and animal bones. The cairn is dated to 2900 BCE.

Taversoe Tuick Chambered Cairn[20]

- Off the B9065 on the Isle of Rousay. (HY 426 276) Signposted.
- An Orkney-style with a rare feature: 2 chambers built one on top of the other, each with its own entrance. A compartmented mini-tomb (1.5m long) is located on the edge of the cairn platform. Bowls, disc beads, and a broken macehead were found in the cairn.

Midhowe Chambered Cairn

- Off the B9064 on Rousay. (HY 371 306) Signposted.
- This Orkney style cairn is very large, with a 12-compartmented chamber over 23 metres long. The cairn itself is ob-

---

[20] At the ***Isbister Chambered Cairn***, on the SE side of South Ronaldsay, 5 miles south of St. Margaret's Hope, (ND 409 845) is the ***Tomb of the Eagles***. The chamber and 3 side-cells of this cairn contained the remains of about 340 human burials, but the popular name of the cairn comes from the discovery of a number of bones and talons from white-tailed sea eagles, perhaps a totem of these people. The site has restricted access; guided tours and a visitor centre.

long and unusually constructed in a herringbone slab pattern.
- Some of the chamber compartments have low stone benches on or under which burials were placed.

Holm of Papa Westry
- (A small uninhabited island) (HY 509 518)
- There are 2, possibly 3, chambered cairns at opposite ends of the island. One is a Maes Howe type with 14 side-cells, and decorated stones, with a concrete roof. The other has 4 chamber compartments and a cell off the end. The island also has a prehistoric settlement, Knap of Howar.

Quoyness Chambered Cairn
- Off the B9069, 4 miles east of Kettletoft, on the Isle of Sanday. (HY 677 377) Footpath is signposted.

- This is a fine Maes Howe style cairn having a large central chamber and 6 side-cells. The cairn is set on a raised platform. Excavation revealed a cist in the chamber floor, and human bones.

Quanterness – on Orkney Mainland (HY 418 120)
- There are 6 side-cells off the main chamber of this 30-metre in diameter cairn. Dated at before 3000 BCE, it is an old monument, built on the north slope of Wideford Hill.

Holland Standing Stone – North Ronaldsay (HY 752 529)
- Over 4 metres high, and perforated by a hole about halfway up.

Wideford Hill Chambered Cairn
- On the mainland off the A965, 2 miles west of Kirkwall. (HY 409 122) Signposted but a long walk.

- A Maes Howe-type cairn with a rectangular chamber and 3 side-cells, within a circular mound.

Brochs:
- *Gurness* (HY 381 268) Used by Picts & Vikings.
- *Burrian* (HY 762 513) Shore-side
- *Borwick* (HY 224 167)
- *Borroughtston* (HY 540 210) On Shapinsay.

Sites on the Shetland Isles:

Westings Hill Stone Circle
- At Tingwall, 5¼ miles NW of Lerwick; an easy walk. (HU 406 460)
- An oval circle of low and fallen boulders, all less than 3" high. Recognizable but hard to spot.

Loch of Strom Stone Circle

- 1.5 miles north of Haggeston, 7 miles NNW of Lerwick, just west of the road; easy access. (HU 403 501)
- A small ellipse near the loch. 7 low stones, and a 4' high stone at the south end. Also 3 fallen stones.

Vementry Chambered Cairn

- On a small island off the west coast of the mainland. (HU 295 609)
- The circular cairn is at the summit of Muckle Ward hill. Set on a platform; the chamber is tripartite, at the end of a long passage.

Punds Water Chambered Cairn

- On a moor near Northmavine, on the mainland. (HU 324 712)
- A kerbed cairn with a tripartite chamber, in good condition.

The Giant's Stones
- On moorland just east of Hamnavoe, on the mainland. (HU 243 805)
- 2 standing stones about 20 metres apart.

Haltadans Stone Circle
- Of uncertain age; it may not be ancient. Located on Fetlar Island, 2¾ miles E of Ugasta pier, 1 mile N of Houbie, a 1 mile ENE walk from North Dale. (HU 622 923)
- A 37' ring of 22 boulders surrounding an earthen circle about 26' across with an entrance at the SW. In the centre are 2 tall stones. 550 yards NNW are 3 kerbed cairns known as the Fiddler's Crus. (Enclosure).

Brochs:
- *Clickhimin* (HU 464 408) Island setting of prehistoric buildings.
- *Mousa* (HU 457 236) Spectacular example.

- *Jarlshof Settlement* (HU 398 095) Prehistoric.
- *Scatness* (HU 390 106) Broch and settlement.
- *Burland* (HU 445 360) Perilous site.
- *Culswick* (HU 253 448) On Easter Skeld.
- *Clumlie* (HU 404 181) Sumburgh.

Aberdeen-shire

East-West differences in Scotland are as distinct as North-South divides. Doric is the local language/dialect of the East, having place-names mostly incomprehensible to Gaelic speakers. The East's traditional music, outlooks and livelihoods, landscape and weather, all differ interestingly from those of the Highlands.

Aberdeen-shire is a farming and fishing region, also reliant on the North Sea oil industry. Unlike West Coast crofting, farming in the East is larger scale and on fertile ground. The hills here are less craggy and close-folded; instead of mist there is haar – fog that rolls inland from the cold North Sea.

But the East Coast is known for getting the lion's share of Scotland's sunshine, and long sand beaches on which to enjoy it. The region has castles, harbours, bird-rich coastal cliffs and midge-free camping. Aberdeen – the granite city – is a busy centre with all the usual urban services and accommodations; smaller villages offer a more relaxed pause.

Prehistorically speaking, (Late Neolithic and Early Bronze Age), Aberdeen-shire brims with sites – dozens of stone circles of a style termed "recumbent" by archaeologists. This style is characterized by a large levelled recumbent stone flanked by tall uprights usually set in the SW arc of the circle. This circle usually contains a kerbed ring-cairn containing cremations; also features a platform with scattered quartz; an alignment on the major southern moonset; gradated stones; and cup marks on the arc of stones that includes the recumbent. Aberdeen-shire is the heartland of this style of monument.

These circles of Northeast Scotland are remarkable in their conformity. The preponderance of granite in their construction is hardly surprising; it would seem the land is built on a uniform foundation of that rock; but the pattern and usage of the recumbent form, and the recurring patterns within that form, are amazingly consistent.

The fact that the recumbent in so many cases differs in rock type from the other circle stones is interesting. Some of these alternate types could only have been found at considerable distance from the desired site. This coupled with the fact that in every case the recumbent is far and away the largest stone of the group means that no part of the undertaking was considered lightly. Seasonal changes undoubtedly were charted through the positioning of the stones, but this in itself is not adequate justification for the amount of industry involved. Agrarian communities need to know the pattern of the seasons, but with similarly oriented groups in such proximity – in the case of Loanhead, there are no less than three other circles within a mile – there has to be another, and in all likelihood, more compelling, reason for their construction.

Recumbent circles rarely occur outside the Northeast area. Intriguingly, however, they constitute the dominant form in one other area, and that area is not in Scotland at all, but in the Southwest of Ireland. A line drawn on the map of Ireland and

Scotland, running from the craggy coast of Cork and Kerry northeastwards and extending as far as the North Sea coast of Scotland, gives an instant identification of the distribution of recumbent circles. The structures may be found anywhere along this (broad) line, but occur in great number at each extremity. These extremities have obvious similarities: they are coastal areas; the land is suited to farming, therefore constitutes – then as now – desirable areas of settlement. The people gradually abandoned their hunter-gatherer lifestyle and began to form communities, and this had a dramatic effect on the landscape and on attitudes toward the land. Investments of time, sweat, and blood in an area of land moves the settler toward attitudes of defence and improvement. Community occupancy provides a reservoir of skills, and of labour which, in allowing the undertaking of grander projects, lead in turn to greater personal and communal investment in the land.

Early farmers, raising crops and livestock on this rich land, certainly had good reason to track the cycles of the seasons, but would they really need such a surfeit of calendars? After all, it is extremely unlikely that the circles, which have endured the millennia, represent the totality of those constructed, yet we can find even these survivors occurring in remarkable concentrations; and each circle represents a sacrifice of time and energy. Time and energy, which was diverted from planting, tending, and harvesting.

And why recumbents? Why should this class be represented so strongly at either end of this line, which cuts across Ireland and Scotland, while rarely occurring elsewhere along the line, and not at all any distance from it? The Scottish recumbents share the features of their Irish counterparts, yet these features are arranged intriguingly at variance. In Scotland, we find the recumbent itself – usually a rock type distinct from that of its flankers – situated at the SSW of the ring; the twin flankers adjacent to the recumbent are the tallest stones in the circle, and the height of the remaining stones diminishes towards the NNE. When we look at the typical Irish recumbent circle, we find the recumbent similarly located, though closer to SW than SSW. But here the recumbent is not placed between the tallest stones of the circle. Instead, it lies opposite them. In the Irish circles, the paired tall stones are called the "portals" and they stand on the NE perimeter. From the portals, the size of the stones falls away, so that the *smallest* stones of the circle are those flanking the recumbent.

So, in both cases the recumbent sits in a comparable position on the circle, aligned to solar or lunar events. In Scotland the lunar observation is favoured. It is fascinating that these circles, occurring as they do at the coastal extremes of this line, are constructed as mirror images; the recumbent defining the axes and orientation, but the remaining stones face portal to flanker, and the smallest stones face out to sea.[21]

---

[21] On the way from Inverness to Aberdeen-shire the traveller passes through the *Moray* region, which has several stone circles: *Innesmill*, (NJ 289 641) 4½ miles ENE of Elgin, which is a possible recumbent ruin; and *Templestone*, (NJ 068 568) 2¼ miles SE of Forres, which appears to be a 4-Poster with a small cairn in the centre. The Pictish *Sueno's Stone*

Banffshire is an area with monuments influenced by the Inverness-shire style of Clava-cairns on one hand, and by the Aberdeen-shire tradition of recumbent circles on the other. Some of the Banffshire monuments include:

Rothiemay Circle
- ¼ mile N of Milltown, 5½ miles N of Huntly; in a field just south of the B9117. (NJ 550 487)
- A ruined recumbent circle once about 92' across; 4 tall stones and the recumbent remain of the original 12. The recumbent is huge – 14' long by 4' thick and 5' tall, and has over 100 cup-marks on its inner face. A stone east of the recumbent is also decorated.
- *Alignments:* The pillar is lined to the major southern moonrise; there may be a midwin-

---

(NJ 046 595) is also a point of interest, as is the ***Auchorachan Standing Stone***, and the ***Sculptor's Cave*** (at Covesea) with its Pictish symbols.

ter sunset alignment through the centre of the recumbent.
- *Type of Stone*: The recumbent is basalt, weighing 20 tons.
- *Condition*: Recognizable.

Marionburgh Circle
- 9 miles WSW of Dufftown, ¾ miles NE of Upper Lagmore. (NJ 183 364) A 300 yard walk.
- A circle 75' across, with 5 standing and 4 fallen stones, ranging from 2'3" (SW) to 9' (SSW) in height. There is a low cairn in the centre.

Upper Lagmore Circle
- A half-mile W of Bridge of Avon; an uphill walk a quarter-mile through a field. (NJ 176 358)
- A ruined Clava-style circle and passage-grave. 5 out of 9 stones still stand, the tallest (W) at 7'3". The SE fallen stone is 12' long.

The passage in the cairn leads to the south side of the central chamber; the entrance faces SSE. The remains of Lower Lagmore Circle are 300 yards to the east.

- *Type of Stone*: Quartzose schist.
- *Condition*: Recognizable.

North Burreldales Circle

- 3½ miles NE of Aberchirder, 4½ miles NW of Turrif. (NJ 676 549) A quarter-mile walk W of the B921.
- Only 2 stones remain standing in this small circle, possibly a 4-Poster, in a grove of trees.

St. Marnan's Chair – (NJ 597 502)

- Standing stone.

Aberdeen-shire Tour of Sites

Loanhead of Daviot

A quarter-mile NW of Daviot, off the B9001, 5 miles NW of Inverurie. (NJ 747 288) Signposted; easy access.

Loanhead, like most recumbent circles, occupies a hillside terrace, but its open views are now obscured on several sides by trees. Despite this it has an expansive feel, enhanced by multiple arrangements at the site. Located on the edge of the village of Daviot, Loanhead seems part of the town.

The monument was built on a man-made platform on a northern slope, and comprises a recumbent circle and a cremation cemetery side-by-side. Just to the northwest of the terrace are some stones engraved with cupmarks. There are other circles in the area, to the north and southeast.

Inside the circle is a kerbed ring-cairn in which were found charcoal, cremated bone, and sherds of earthenware. Some of these artifacts suggest that the circle may belong to the period just after 3000 BCE, with the ring-cairn a later addition and the cremation cemetery belonging to a later period still.

The circle consists of 8 stones and of course the recumbent grouping of 3 stones. The recumbent in this case has been fractured, presumably by frost, and appears as two "wafers". The ring has a diameter of 68'.

The ring-cairn has a kerbed diameter of 54' and a central space of 13'. In the excavations of 1932 it was observed that a fire had been burned in the interior of the circle before the ring-cairn was built.

Each circle stone stands on its own little "cairn" and beneath these cairns were found small pits containing charcoal and fragments of flat-rimmed ware. On the inner face of the stone to the east of the eastern flanker are 12 cup-marks and these have astronomical significance in a rather unusual manner for a recumbent group. A line of sight from the centre, touching on the eastern side of this engraved stone, has an azimuth of 139° and a declination of –23.8° - for midwinter sunrise. Loanhead has its lunar observation too.

Old Keig

1 mile west of Keig, 2-3 miles NNE of Alford. (NJ 597 194) Short walk.

Old Keig is not signposted, and took us some time to find – though once on the correct route the monument can be spotted – just – from the road. One of the reasons this site is so appealing is because it is not tended or enclosed. It stands on a wooded ridge overlooking farmland hills and fields of grazing cattle.

The site, which once included a ring-cairn, is hummocky and overgrown, but seems natural rather than just neglected, despite the ruined configuration and missing stones; the site still gives an impression of containing a circle.

The monument is established on a terrace on rising ground commanding a view to the southwest, and an avenue of mature beech trees joins circle and road. On each side of this avenue are farm fields. The circle is estimated to have been 82' across, and however many stones once constituted the ring, there are now only the recumbent, its flankers, and an easterly stone marking the southwestern arc – though there is a grouping of 3 small stones to the west of this. The remains of the circle lie within a bank which, although now low, appears to be about 10' wide.

The surviving stones are massive. The western flanker is 8'10" high; the eastern is 9'6". The recumbent is a whopping 16' long, 6'9" high, and 6' thick, estimated to weigh over 40 tons! This recumbent is not of local stone, but of sillimanite gneiss, the closest source of which is several miles to the southeast. Like most recumbent circles, this site appears to be aligned to the major southern moonset.

Inside the circle there is evidence that the turf was stripped away and a fire of hazel, birch, willow, alder, and oak had been set; interesting, because these were the sacred trees of the Celts as well. On top of the ashes a kerbed ring-cairn was built, of 61' in diameter, with a 15' central space. In the central space a pit was found in which were the remains of cremated bones and charcoal. Also sherds of flat-rimmed ware and Beaker ware. Flints and a small lignite armlet completed the finds.

Cullerie Stone Circle

>13 miles west of Aberdeen, off the A944, 4.5 miles NW of Petercoulter. (NJ 785 043)

Surprising for northeast circles – which usually stand on hillside terraces – Cullerie is in a low boggy area. The site was levelled, then a ring of willow laid down and burned. 7 compact cairns were built over these ashes, around a double-kerbed centre cairn. Oak and hazel charcoal, and cremated bones, were placed inside the rings which were then in-filled with small stones. Each tiny cairn is kerbed by 11 stones (a single exception has only 9). A very tidy monument.

Many recumbent sites were prepared by burning willow and other significant woods. The choice of woods, like the choice of stones, was not based on convenience. The 33' circle around the Cullerie cairns is a true circle, of 8 red granite boulders brought from higher ground. The boulders rise in height toward the north. They are seated in a gravel bed, but over time acidic peat eroded their lower parts. Cullerie seemed a place of both death and vitality, like a perpetual motion machine made of stone: a paradox.

Easter Aquorthies

2-3 miles west of Inverurie (NJ 732 208)

Easy access (short walk). Signposts.

Easter Aquorthies (possible The Field of Worship) has information boards at the car park and at the site. It is certainly a very pretty circle, though a little too manicured for my tastes. Nonetheless impressive. The stones are of different types: porphyry, granite, jasper; they form a remarkably colourful circle.

The granite hues range from the east's dramatic red jasper and pale sunrise pink, to the west's deep twilight greys and the tall flankers' lighter greys. The majestic recumbent is ruddy granite with quartz striations. Two heavy blocking stones placed at right angles to the recumbent support it on the inner side, and one of them has a deep green cast to it, veined with quartz. These right angle stones create an "alcove" at the recumbent.

The ring stands inside a low earthwork and is a slightly flattened circle of 61' by 59', aligned WNW-ESE. The flankers are 7'6" in height; the recumbent is 12'6" long and 4'6" high. It appears that the circle stones were erected in opposing pairs with a single, smallest stone to the NNE. The stones are clearly gradated, increasing in height from the NNE round either side to the flankers; a very symmetrical arrangement. There is an interior mound with a slightly hollowed centre in which is a capstoned cist – probably this was the remains of a ring cairn.

Interested to check similarities with other recumbent circles we'd seen, it was fascinating to find that at this circle also there is a stone roughly marking west, in this case a small stone embedded in the banking between 2 larger standing stones. From the centre of the circle, looking over this western marker, the observer is looking directly to the dramatic peak of Mither Tap, an unusually well-defined summit of Benachie, the highest hill in the area.

Tomnaverie Circle

4 miles NW of Aboyne, ¾ miles SE of Tarland, off the B9044. (NJ 486 034) Signposted; easy access.

Tomnaverie rates high for natural location. The knoll it perches on was certainly not the easiest place on which to build a stone monument, but the view is panoramic. Visiting the site in 1996 was complicated but not arduous: we opened and closed a gate in order to bring our vehicle up to the quarry, at which point we found ourselves – even before exiting the car – surrounded by large, interested cattle. The walk to the site was through a herd of these muddy beasts – including a bull.

The site itself, enclosed by a fence, has never been excavated. It consists of the remains of a recumbent circle built sometime between 1800 BCE and 1600 BCE, so is not as old as some. The countryside around it is fertile land through which rivers lazily wind and farms prosper.

Tomnaverie is a funny circle – more a jumble – of standing stones irregularly spaced, some very small or half-buried in turf, remains of cairns perhaps. The recumbent and its attendants anchor the configuration.

Returning to Tomnaverie in 2001, I was dismayed at the site's further degradation by the adjacent quarry, which had advanced to the very borders of the circle. The site's bleak state was amplified by the January day's fogged-in grey chill, the wet snow that began falling as we got out of the car, and the naked rubble of frozen mud and stone surrounding the place. The cows – and bull – were still there, but little else could be seen of land or sky that day, and it was sharply cold.

On the plus side, this site is easily found, well signposted and close to the road. On the negative side, the quarrying has taken place so close to the circle as to literally undermine it.

Originally, the ring would have been 61' across; about 9 stones remain along with the recumbent and its flankers. The rock used is the local red granite; the recumbent is basalt, a much heavier, denser rock. Inside, the ring-cairn would have been about 48' across; the kerbs are to some degree extant though many are displaced and the inner space of the cairn is indistinguishable from the clutter and jumble.

Again, at Tomnaverie, was the existence of a short grouping of small uprights arrayed side-by-side, forming a section of the greater arc just west of the recumbent and west flanker. The north and south circle stones seemed particularly "characterful" and important also, though not necessarily bigger or heavier than their neighbours. A subjective opinion, but they seemed significant stones.

Additional Sites

Aberdeen-shire circles were almost all built between circa 2700 BCE and 2000 BCE.

Backhill of Drachlaw
- 2¾ miles ESE of Inverkeithny, 4 miles SW of Turriff. (NJ 673 464) Walk 150 yards N of a farm track. Easy access.
- An elliptical circle of 5 hefty, gradated stones, with an even heftier block 6'9" long by 3' wide, at the NW. 300 yards NE is Cairn Riv with its huge "Hag's Stone" by the B9024. This stone is 8'6" high; its girth is 26'10" and it weighs over 14 tons. It is flanked by 2 smaller stones. Bronze-Age ar-

tifacts were reported to have been found in or near the circle.
- *Type of Stone*: Dark basalt with veins and pebbles of quartz.
- *Condition*: Good.

Arnhill Circle
- 2 miles SE of Ruthven, 3½ miles N of Huntly. (NJ 531 456) Walk 250 yards W of the B9022.
- Only the recumbent is left, but it weighs about 16 tons, is 11'9" long, 5' high, and is balanced on blocks.
- *Alignments*: A set of concentric circles carved on the rock mark the position of the major southern moonset.

Yonder Bognie Wardend Circle
- 1¾ miles WSW of Inverkeithny, 5¾ miles NE of Huntly. (NJ 601 458) Walk a quarter-mile S of Yonder Bognie farm. Easy access.

- This is a family-maintained ring with 4 standing and 2 fallen stones, on a slope. The substantial recumbent and flankers are interestingly *within* the circumference of the circle.
- *Alignments:* The recumbent is aligned with Colyne Hill and the major southern moonrise.
- *Artifacts*: A deep layer of pulverized bone, broken sherds, and burnt matter under the paved area of the central space.
- *Condition*: Recognizable.

Raich Circle

- 2¼ miles S of Inverkeithny, 6 miles ENE of Huntly. (NJ 618 436) Take the distillery lane SW for a half-mile. Walk 100 yards S through the field.
- A transitional-style ring – perhaps a 4-Poster – on a raised mound. Made up of low stones, some of them fallen. The tallest 2 stones are on the SE at 4'8" and the NNW at 4'4".

- *Condition*: Recognizable.

Logie Newton Circle
- 4¼ miles NW of Rothienorman, 8 miles E of Huntly. (NJ 657 392) Walk a half-mile WNW uphill.
- 3 ruinous small rings, with round cairns; the circles are notable for being made of stunning white quartz blocks.
- *Artifacts*: An urn was found containing human bones.

Berrybrae Circle
- 5 miles ENE of Strichen, 6.5 miles SSE of Fraserburgh. (NK 028 572) Just SW of the lane junction; easy access.
- A 9-stone plus recumbent ellipse built onto a raised platform cut into the hillside. In front of the 10'10" recumbent was a cobbled platform strewn with white quartz. There is a kerbed ring-cairn in the centre. Sometime around 1760 BCE the circle and cairn were

deliberately smashed; the cobbles were used to build a thick wall around the wrecked ellipse. Urn sherds were then placed in a niche in this wall, beside a beaker, both offerings covered by the wall's clay capping. In the 19th century a grove of trees was planted around the looted, ruined site.

- *Alignments*: the hump on the recumbent stone points to the moon's minor setting.
- *Artifacts*: Cremated human bones found in the ring-cairn.
- *Type of Stone*: The recumbent is basalt.
- *Condition*: Restored.

Aikey Brae Circle

- 1¼ miles WSW of Old Deer, 10¼ miles N of Ellon. On Parkhouse Hill a quarter-mile east of the farm (NJ 959 471) Easy access.
- A banked recumbent circle of gradated stones (4'7" – 7'3") 47' across. 9 out of 10 stones, plus the recumbent, remain, though

several have fallen. The recumbent is a 21 tons stone, 14'9" long by 4'3" high.
- *Alignment*: Major southern moonset.
- *Condition*: Recognizable.

South Ythsie Circle
- ¾ miles WSW of Tarves, 4½ miles W of Ellon. (NJ 884 305) Walk 250 yards E from a lane just S of the trees. Easy access.
- 6 substantial stones make up what may be a transitional 4-Poster that once stood on a mound with a central hollow and single kerb-stone. The 4 tallest stones form a rectangle. This ring is only a half-mile south of a 4-Poster at Shethin.
- *Condition*: Good.

Kirkton of Bourtie Circle
- 1½ miles S of Old Meldrum, 2¼ miles NE of Inverurie. (NJ 801 250) Walk N 200 yards from the lane; easy access.

- A ruined recumbent circle; only the recumbent, east flanker, and 2 western stones remain, but the flanker is a tall 9'10" and the recumbent stretches 17' and weighs about 30 tons! The western stones are 6' and 7'9" tall. Cairn remains are dispersed within the circle.
- *Alignments*: to the major southern moonset.
- *Type of Stone*: Local grey granite.
- *Condition*: Recognizable.

Hatton of Ardoyne Circle
- 1¼ miles SE of Old Rayne, 2 miles SE of Insch. (NJ 659 268) A quarter-mile walk east from Ardoyne farm; easy access.
- An 84' circle with 9 out of 13 stones still standing, from 4' to 6' tall. The recumbent is narrow and flat-topped; in front of it is a stone platform. The contained ring-cairn is kerbed and set 2' into the ground, with a large (64') kerbed central space.

- *Artifacts*: 2 rectangular graves paved with small stones, containing cremated bones and burnt urn sherds.
- *Type of Stone*: Light grey granite recumbent and flankers (stone from across the valley) and the other stones of local metamorphic gneiss.
- *Condition*: Recognizable.

Ardlair Circle
- ¾ miles S of Kennethmont station, 5 miles W of Insch. (NJ 552 279) A quarter-mile walk SW of the farm.
- A round cairn surrounded by a ring in which only the recumbent, flankers, and 1 other stone remain. 2 slabs jut out from the recumbent, as at Easter Aquorthies.
- *Artifacts*: A wrecked cist, cremated bone and charcoal.
- *Condition*: Recognizable.

Cothiemuir Wood Circle
- ½ miles NE of Keig, 5¼ miles SSW of Insch. (NJ 617 198) A short walk from a lane through trees.
- An incomplete but still good recumbent circle 75' across. The recumbent is 13'8" long and has 2 very striking, tall flankers. The recumbent rests on a square granite block. There are possible cup marks on the recumbent. At the circle's centre is a large granite block covering a small pit.
- *Alignments*: the west flanker aligns with the major southern moonset.
- *Type of Stones*: Red and grey granite; the recumbent is basalt.
- *Condition*: Recognizable.

North Strone Circle
- 1½ miles SSE of Alford, 2 miles WNW of Kirkton. (NJ 584 138) Walk from Guise farm a half-mile NW, uphill.

- Wee stones make up this 65' circle; even the recumbent is tiny for its role; 4'9" long, 1'6" thick, 2'7" high – if it were still upright.
- *Alignments*: To the major southern moonset.
- *Artifacts*: Under interior pavement stones were 7 graves with some human remains, flints, and Bronze Age urn shards.
- *Type of Stone*: 10 stones of white quartz-porphyries, 4 stones of pink granite, 2 of grey granite.
- *Condition*: Restored.

Whitehill Circle
- 2¼ miles WSW of Monymusk, 4½ miles ESE of Alford. (NJ 678 505) Take the forestry track W for a mile. Walk a quarter-mile N through trees.
- A 72' diameter recumbent circle with a large kerbed ring-cairn. The east flanker has fallen; the west is a tall stone. The cairn's centre is an irregularly shaped open space.

There are small cairns also, outside the circle.
- *Type of Stone*: Reddish quartz porphyry circle stones; dark grey recumbent veined with quartz.
- *Condition*: Recognizable.

Deer Park Circle
- A half-mile N of Monymusk, 3 miles W of Kemnay. (NJ 684 156) Walk 100 yards E of lane; easy access.
- A 4-Poster – unusual for the area – on a terrace overlooking the River Don. 3 thick stones remain, the tallest of which is 5'2". The circle's diameter is only 15'4". There are 4 major recumbent circles within a few miles of this site.

Castle Fraser Circle
- 2.5 miles SSW of Kemnay, 6.5 miles SSW of Inverurie. (NJ 715 125) Easy access from a side-lane.

- 6 out of 10 gradated stones stand on a levelled terrace; the recumbent and tall flankers are among the intact stones. A ring-cairn is within, and 727' to the east is a pair of 7 ft. standing stones 48' apart from one another. A mile and a half to the NNE is an 11'6" standing stone.
- *Alignments*: Lined up to the major southern moonset.
- *Artifacts*: Sherds of a "thick and massive urn," cremated bones and charcoal.
- *Condition*: Good.

Sunhoney Circle

- 1½ miles W of Echt, 8½ miles WNW of Petercoulter. (NJ 716 058) Walk a quarter-mile north and west from Sunhoney farm. Easy access.
- A fallen 14'9" recumbent with 31 cup-marks is part of an 11-stone circle. The ring is 83'3" in diameter; the flankers

are 7'6" and 6'7" tall. Inside is a ring-cairn with a kerbed central space.
- *Alignments*: Between Meikle Tap and Greymore, where the southern moon at its minor setting descends.
- *Artifacts*: 8 deposits of cremated bone, and a cist with sherds.
- *Type of Stone*: Red granite and gneiss; the recumbent is a thin slab of grey granite.
- *Condition*: Fair.

Dyce Circle
- 1¾ miles W of Dyce, 7¼ miles SE of Inverurie. (NJ 860 133) A quarter-mile walk uphill NW of Dyce farm.
- On a hillside with fine views, this is a wonderful, if ruined, circle of 10 stones ranging from 4'4" to the tall flankers at 9'6" and 11' high. The recumbent weighs 24 tons, is 10' long and 10'6" high – extremely tall for a recumbent; and instead of a flat top, it is

peaked. Inside the circle are remains of a ring-cairn.
- *Type of Stone*: Red granite; the recumbent is darker granite.
- *Condition*: Good.

Balquhain Circle
- 1 mile E of Chapel of Garioch, 3 miles NW of Inverurie. (NJ 735 241) A quarter-mile walk across fields W of the A96; wall and fence obstacles.
- 3 stones and the recumbent remain of the 12 originals in the 68' diameter circle. The recumbent is 12'6" long by 5'11" tall. There are cup-marks on the fallen east flanker and on the west flanker.
- *Alignments*: the east flanker was aligned with the most southerly moonrise. There is also a stone aligned to the minor moonset several degrees north of SW.
- *Type of Stone*: Red granite, quartzite, basalt, the recumbent is white-grained granite.

- There is an outlier 10'3" tall, of quartz, to the SE.
- *Condition*: Recognizable.

Other Additional Sites

- *Broomend of Crichie Circle* (NJ 779 196) Ruined circle-henge.
- *Longman Hill Barrow* (NJ 737 620) 70 meter earth mound.
- *Loudin Wood Circle* (NJ 962 497) Difficult to find.
- *Memsie Cairn* (NJ 976 620) Huge Bronze Age cairn.
- *Midmar Kirk Circle* (NJ 699 064) Christianised.
- *Old Rayne Circle* (NJ 679 280) Badly ruined.
- *Shethin Tarves Circle* (NJ 882 328) Small, ruined site.
- *Strichen Circle* (NJ 936 544) Severely disrupted.

- *Tomnagorn Circle* (NJ 651 077) Fair condition.
- *Tullos Hill Cairns* (NJ 959 041) Remains of 4 cairns.
- *West Cults Cairn* (NJ 883 027) Impressive cairn.
- *Whitehill Wood Circle* (NJ 678 505) Damaged, overgrown.
- *Wormy Hillock Henge* (NJ 449 307) Small but well preserved.

Kincardine-shire Sites:

Auchquhorthies

 4¾ miles ESE of Petercoulter, 7 miles SSW of Aberdeen, on the W of the A92. (NO 901 963) Walk 200 yards N of Aquorthies Farm on the farm lane. Easy access.

2 recumbent circles 330 yards apart, of a complex of 4 rings on a line 1¼ miles long. A

Clava-style ring cairn lies to the north of the recumbents, with a 4-Poster beyond that. The Auchquhorthies circle stands on a levelled platform and is 75' in diameter. The outer circle has 10 standing and 2 fallen stones remaining of 28. the stones are gradated, and the recumbent is a 9'9" long, 5' high block. Only its western flanker remains, at 6' tall. As a "variant recumbent", the recumbent stone is east of south and within the circle's perimeter. A kerbed ring cairn is linked to the recumbent by a long slab.

Alignment: To the major southern moonrise.

Artifacts: Charcoal, cremated bone, sherds, possibly a cist.

Type of Stone: Reddish granite; the recumbent and flankers are greyish granite streaked with quartz.

Condition: Recognizable.

Garrol Wood (also, the Nine Stones)

3½ miles SE of Banchory, 9½ miles WNW of Stonehaven. (NO 723 912) Walk 100 meters E from a forest track. The West Mulloch circles: Esslie the Greater and Esslie the Lesser, are N and NW of Garrol Wood. A uniquely aberrant recumbent circle; an ellipse of stones with rough walling between them. The recumbent and flankers are within the ellipse, and the recumbent is 7'6" long but only 3'9" high. The flankers are 5' and 6'8" tall. The ring-cairn within the circle is a mess, very oddly configured, but its central space (about 12'6" across) is lined with 6 (once 7) carefully gradated tall slabs. There was a pit in the centre. A stony platform links the recumbent stone with the ring-cairn.

Artifacts: Cremated adult bones, charcoal, urn sherds.

Type of Stone: Reddish granite; the recumbent may be diorite.

Condition: Recognizable.

Glassel

2 miles SE of Torphins, 4 miles NW of Banchory. (NO 649 997) Hidden in a wood just west of the lane.

A mini 4-Poster; a circle only 12'6" across, of 5 low stones forming a rectangle. A sandstone slab lies near the northern stones and beyond that is a granite slab that may've capped a cist. There is a low outlier to the SE.

Artifacts: flint flakes and charcoal.
Condition: Good.

Raedykes

¼ mile NW of West Raedykes, 3½ miles NW of Stonehaven. (NO 832 906) A quarter-mile walk from the farm; easy access. 4 ring-cairns are situated over a 102-yard bent line. In the NW a ruined stone circle encloses a kerbed ring-cairn. 60 yards to the SSE is a ring-cairn with no surrounding circle; 17 yards to its east is a similar configuration. At the SE is a ring-cairn with 8 of its circle stones still standing, and a ruined kerbed cairn.

Condition: Recognizable.

Additional Sites:
- *Cairnfauld Stone Circle* (NO 754 941) Possible recumbent.
- *Cairnwell Stone Circle* (NO 907 974) Clava ring-cairn, ruined.
- *Cape Long Barrows* (NO 633 644)
- *Craighead Badentoy Stone Circle* (NO 912 977) Disrupted.
- *Esslie the Greater Stone Circle* (NO 717 916) Overgrown recumbent.
- *Esslie the Lesser Stone Circle* (NO 722 921) Recumbent remains.
- *Old Bourtreebush Stone circle* (NO 903 961) Partial recumbent ring.

Angus Sites:

Angus has a few small, often ruinous, Bronze Age rings; ***Balkemback***, (NO 382 384), 4.5 miles north of Dundee, which may be the ruins of a 4-Poster whose stones are packed with cup-and-ring markings, is the best of the Angus circles. There is a broch – ***Laws Hill*** – at (NO 491 349), built within a fort; and Celtic crosses at ***St. Vigeans*** (NO 638 429) and ***Meigle***, (NO 287 445), and the Pictish ***Aberlemno Stone*** at (NO 522 555).

Perthshire

Perthshire seems to draw harmonious features of many other regions of Scotland together into a grace of landscape, distinct in its own way. It has lonely moors, rich pastures and stately trees, fast rivers and hills rising into rocky outcrops, and croplands presided over by pheasants. Buzzards cruise the uplands; lochs glimmer under a sky that generally seems to offer gentler weather than that on the coasts.

What characterizes Perthshire most may be its wealth of stone buildings: stone houses, stone barns, stone walls, stone churches, stone castles, a seemingly endless collection of stone manors, and of course, stone circles.

The style of these Perthshire circles is mainly the "4-Poster" though you'll also find some large ovals, 6-stone circles, and even a few "variant recumbents." Many of the sites require a determined search or hike to reach; others are located by (or in one case divided by) a road or farm track.

Much of Perthshire is rural; many B&Bs, country hotels, self-catering cottages, camping, and a few hostels. Perth is the largest town and transportation hub, and has a range of accommodations and services.

Lundin Farm Stone Circle

Go south from Pitlochrey on the A9 and exit onto the A827 toward Aberfeldy. About 1¾ miles before reaching Aberfeldy, turn left at a small hand-lettered sign reading "Lundin," and drive a short way on the lane. (NN 882 505). Park and walk a quarter-mile on the dirt track SE, just past the farmhouse. An easy walk.

This circle is a 4-Poster of large quartziferous schist stones enclosing a small area. On the right on the approach to the circle is a prominent stone that may be an outlier. The site itself is a raised mound surrounded by fields, looking to Ben Lawers in the west. An oak tree shelters the stones, lichened trunk and lichened stones now the same colour. There is a peacefulness about the monument. The tallest stone, at the NE, is 7'3"; each of the 4 stones is different in shape and character.

Excavation of the mound revealed cremated bone and Bronze Age potsherds in a hollow at its summit. A little ways beyond the mound to the SE lies a prostrated slab that, when erect, would have aligned with midwinter sunrise. The slab is adorned with 43 cup-marks, most of them moss-filled now as the stone gradually becomes integrated into the ground on which it lies.

A second 4-Poster used to stand 80 yards north of this site.

There is a standing stone surrounded by a large circle of holly bushes – and a fence – in the farmyard itself, near the bottom of the lane. The stone appears to align with the outlier and site above.

Continuing on the A827 through Aberfeldy, and turning onto the B846, you'll pass the ***Carse Farm North*** stone circle (NN 802 488) 3½ miles west of Aberfeldy, on your left (south). Look sharp for Carse Farm, then the circle which is in a field not far from the road. The field is often in crop, and there is nowhere to park or even pull over, so this 4-Poster is best seen in passing.

Fortingall

A quarter-mile east of the village of Fortingall on the B846. (NN 747 470) Continue from Carse Farm past Keltnyburn; the site is on the left in a grassy field.

Two 4-Posters and a ruined recumbent variant are neatly clustered in the field. There is little now to distinguish in terms of the original configurations, excavated in 1970. The NE 4-Poster was built with fairly large corner stones, 4 smaller stones between each corner, in a rectangle. At the centre, charcoal and burnt bone was found.

The SW 4-Poster had a small stone between each of its corners, and was of a similar size to its neighbour. In this circle, a flooring of tiny pebbles, several quartz stones, and part of an Iron Age jet ring were excavated.

SE of the 4-Poster is Fortingall south with an unusual setting of 3 (remaining) stones in a 20' line running SE-NW. This may be the remnant of a recumbent variant oriented to the major southern moonset.

In Fortingall itself, beside the hotel, in the churchyard, stands what may be the oldest tree in the world – the famous ***Fortingall Yew***. The roots of this tree, which continues to flourish in a walled enclosure, are around 5,000 years old. It is an amazing thing to gaze at this tree and contemplate the passage of time, events, and civilizations it has witnessed.

Croft Morag Stone Circle

4 miles WSW of Aberfeldy, 2 miles NE of Kenmore. (NN 797 472) From Fortingall continue to Fearnan, turn left onto the A827 through Kenmore.

The beauty of stone in this part of Scotland is apparent in the area's natural artistry of crags.[22] The area also possesses a plethora of baronial mansions. Given all this, we shouldn't be surprised to see a farmhouse sporting a Neolithic circle in its yard.

Forget privacy, visiting this monument. The Croft Morag circle stands close to a busy main road, on its south side; but too tantalizing a monument to pass up.

A hill rises beyond the low ground that croft and circle nestle upon. The farmhouse yard is park-like with fine trees. But the circle itself is at first bewildering; it is no simple arrangement. The modern world's proximity fades as one enters the Neolithic complexity of the monument and the impervious presence of its stones.

The configuration developed in phases beginning around 3000 BCE, with timber posts and a

---

[22] The ***Scottish Crannog Centre*** is located near Kenmore (and Croft Morag) just off the A827 (signposted). At the centre is a fully reconstructed crannog of the late Bronze Age-Early Iron Age period. There is an exhibition, tour, and video; the centre is open daily from April to October.

central boulder where burnt bone was discovered by the investigating archaeologists. The post arrangement was aligned on the major southern moonset, as with Aberdeen-shire circles. These timbers were replaced by 8 boulders of schist, height-gradated from about 2½ to 4½ feet, in a horseshoe configuration. An additional, smaller, stone rests outside the open mouth of this arrangement. The site has yielded various assorted fragments of locally-produced earthenware which can be dated to this period of the site's development.

A 60' kerbed bank surrounds the artificial platform upon which these stones stand. A cup-marked stone, to the NE, aligns with the midsummer sun as it rises over the surrounding hills. A recumbent stone, heavily cup-marked, lies on the kerbed bank, aligning with the southern moonset. The monument's builders, at this phase anyway, must have had connections with counterparts – those recumbent stylists of Northeast Scotland.

If all this complicated aligning and configuring was not enough, the builders decided to splash out with a 40' circle of 12 good-sized stones around the outside of the horseshoe. These circle stones are wonderful: shapely, approachable, inviting touch. Two additional tall pillar stones complete the dazzle, framing an entrance to the ESE. The more northerly of this pair may have marked the equinox sunrises, and the pits discovered at the bases of the pillars may have been graves.

This monument is in superb condition: a treat.

Additional Sites
Parkneuk

- 3½ miles NW of Alyth, 4 miles N of Blairgowrie. (NO 195 515) A quarter-mile walk north of the lane to Heatheryhaugh; fair access.
- A 4-Poster on high ground: 1 stone fallen, the others gradated to the SSW, the tallest 4' high and the lowest at the NNE. The circle is in fair condition. 600 yards to the SSW, on the Hill of Drimmie, is another 4-Poster. 30

yards SSE of Parkneuk is a big glacial boulder with 10 cup-marks. There is also a ruined circle 90 yards SW, with 1 standing and 5 fallen stones.

Ardblair
- 1½ miles SW of Blairgowrie, 4½ NW of Coupar Angus. (NO 160 439) The B947 cuts through the circle: caution, fast traffic.

- An obviously disrupted 6-stone ring, once 48'6" in diameter. The stones are gradated to the SW, to the tallest stone at 5'11". The (moved) west stone is now inside the ring and is 7" high. Several other stones were moved or broken when the road was built. At one time this was a very fine circle.

Monzie
- A quarter-mile SE of Monzie, 2 miles NE of Crieff. (NN 882 243) A short walk west of the Gilmertin-Monzie lane; easy access

- A small kerb-circle with a hollowed centre, in a pasture. 10 low boulders stand side-by-side in a 16'5" circle. The heaviest stones are at the west. There is a gap where stones may have been in the SE, and cup-marks on the SE stone. Cup-marks are also found in abundance on a large fallen slab to the SW of the circle. A cobbled causeway links this stone to the circle. A hazelwood fire was burnt in the ring's centre; pieces of white quartz were scattered around the kerb of a centre cist.
- *Artifacts*: Cremated bones of an adult and a 6 year-old child were found in the cist.
- *Type of Stone*: Granite boulders; the prostrate slab is metamorphosed grit.
- *Condition*: Good.

Tigh-na-Ruaich

- A half-mile north of Ballinluig, 3¾ miles SSE of Pitlochry. (NN 975 535) In a garden beside the road.

- A classic 6-stone ellipse of gradated stones, highest at the SSW where a massive 6'6" high by 7' wide stone leans inwards. The stones all seem to have been planted with their pointed ends downward.
- *Artifacts*: 4 very large urns filed with burnt bone, from what may have been a kerbed cist, were very unprofessionally excavated.
- *Condition*: Good.

Na Carraigean Edintian

- 3 miles SW of Blair Atholl, 4¾ miles W of Killicrankie. (NN 839 620) a 2¾ mile walk through Ailean Forest; arduous and uphill.
- A 4-Poster in a beautifully scenic location. A low kerbed circular mound on which a gradated configuration stands. The tallest stone is only 3'10" high. The centre of the boulder circle is hollowed. Another circle notable for its fine view.
- *Condition*: Good.

Clachan an Diridh

- 3 miles west of Pitlochry, 4½ miles south of Killicrankie. (NN 924 558) Walk 1½ miles from Port na Craig, follow the track into the wood and go SSW for another mile, and west for a quarter-mile. The circle is at the west edge of the wood, in front of Loch na Moine Moire.
- On very high ground, at the rim of a mountain terrace, stands this 4-Poster. The NNW stone is missing; the remaining 3 stones are thin slabs with their faces on a NNE-SSW axis. They range in height from 3'3" (NNE) to 6' (SW). The site is mainly enjoyed for its view.
- *Type of Stone*: Local sandstone.
- *Condition*: Recognizable.

Machuinn

- A half-mile NE of Lawers, 8¼ NE of Killin. Just west of the A827. (NN 682 401) A

quarter-mile walk north over field; easy access.
- 4 heavy stones, 3'7" to 4'10" high, form the western arc of an ellipse on a natural mound overlooking the loch. 2 stones are fallen at the NE; a 4'5" stone stands at the SE. In the south a 6'5" by 5' slab lies prostrate.
- *Condition*: Neglected.

Kinnell

- A half-mile E of Killin, by Kinnell farm, SW of the end of Loch Tay. (NN 576 327) a half-mile walk NE along the farm track; easy access.
- An ellipse of 6 stones gradated from 4' to 6'6" at the SSW. This circle is typical of 6-stone central Scotland configurations.
- *Type of Stone*: Dark grey schist.
- *Condition*: Good.

Other Additional Sites

- *Airlich Stone Circle* (NN 959 386) Difficult access.
- *Bandirran Stone Circle* (NO 207 310) Little-known circle.
- *Clach na Tiompan Stone Circle* (NN 831 329) Spoiled 4-Poster.
- *Craighill Mill Stone Circle* (NO 185 481) 4-Poster with cup-marked outlier.
- *Druid's Seat* (NO 123 313) Ruined circle.
- *Ferntower Stone Circle* (NN 874 226) On a private golf course.
- *Fowlis Wester Stone Circle* (NN 923 249) 2 ruinous rings.
- *Greenland Stone Circle* (NN 767 427) Steep access.
- *Kinloch Stone Circle* (NO 117 475) 4-Poster.
- *Moncreiffe Stone Circle* (NO 132 193) On private grounds.
- *Murthly Stone Circle* (NO 103 386) Badly damaged.

- *Sandy Road West, Scone Stone Circle* (NO 132 265) Paired rings, roadside.
- *St. Madoes Standing Stones* (NO 197 209) 2 cup-marked stones.
- *Tullybeagles Stone Circle* (NO 013 362) Paired rings, ruinous.
- There are Celtic crosses at **Dupplin** (NO 050 189) and **Dunfallandy** (NN 946 565).
- Stirlingshire has brochs at **Coldoch** (NS 696 981) and **Tappoch** (NS 833 849) and a cairn at **Hill of Airthrey** (NS 796 981).

Sites in Other Scottish Regions
Fife Sites:

Balbirnie

¾ miles NW of Markinch, 6½ miles N of Kirkcaldy. (NO 285 029) Just E of the A92, in Balbirnie Park. 260 yards N of North Lodge, alongside the track; easy access.

This circle was excavated and re-erected 120 yards SE of the original site in 1970-71 when the road was widened. The original was built in phases. 10 stones stand in an ellipse – 3 broken and 2 missing – in a large configuration with the tallest (6') at the south. In the centre was a slab-lined rectangle enclosure probably built around 1100 BCE. 4, maybe 5, cists were inserted in the space between stones and enclosure, with a very small cist at the NE. A cist at the east was decorated with cup-and-rings. Just to the south of another cist was a slab with 17 cup-marks. A subsequent phase of use for this site involved cremations.

Alignments: Midsummer sunrise aligned from the centre to the north side of the NE stone.

Artifacts: Many! Cremated bone in the stoneholes, and sherds. Cremated bone in the east cist; cremated bones of a woman and child, and a bone bead, in the small NE cist; cremated remains of another woman and child in the NW cist – also a food vessel and flint knife; a jet button in the SE cist. Other finds include beaker ware and broken urns.

Condition: Restored.

Balfarg

1¼ miles NW of Markinch, 3¼ miles SE of Falkland. (NO 281 032) Turn SE at the roundabout, from the B969. signposted; easy access. Only 330 yards WNW of the Balbirnie Circle, on the other side of the A92.

A restored circle-henge built in phases, with 2 large stones standing WNW-ESE of each other framing the NW causeway of a big horseshoe-shaped ditch and bank. This opens to the WSW at the edge of a gully. The henge is 213' across and originally constructed of a ring of 16 gradated posts in an 82' circle. The 2 heaviest posts stood outside the circle as western portals. Outside and inside this ring were 5 smaller timber configurations which may've supported a concealing palisade. Later, the timber rings were replaced by 2 large concentric, west-gradated stone circles. A pit, probably dating from around 1900 BCE, is near the centre.

Artifacts: Under the henge plateau was broken Neolithic pottery, burnt wood and bone. In the timber postholes, grooved ware, charcoal, and burnt bone was found, dating to about 2900 BCE. In the centre pit, a young man's body was buried with a flint knife and handled beaker.

Condition: Restored.

Lundin Links

1¾ miles NE of Levin, 7¾ miles SSE of Cupar. (NO 404 027) 200 yards E of the lane N to Thomsford, on a private golf course; permission required to visit.

3 very tall stones stand on the golfcourse fairway, in what was a long rectangle similar to some Perthshire sites. The NNE stone is missing. The other stones are a soaring 16'8", 15', and 13'8" tall – this last one (in the SSE) is 6'5" wide. Mighty stones.

Alignment: SSW toward Comrie Hill and the minor southern moonset, and SSE to the minor southern moonrise behind Bass Rock.

Artifacts: Cists, bones, and a possible jet button.

Condition: Recognizable.

Additional Sites:

- *Easter Pitcorthies Standing Stone* (NO 497 039) Single stone, heavily cup-marked.

- *Torry Standing Stone* (NT 029 865) Single cup-marked stone.

Edinburgh Sites:
- *Caiystane Standing Stone* (NT 242 683) Single stone, cup-marked.
- *Newbridge Standing Stones* (NT 123 726) Barrow and 4 standing stones.

East Lothian Sites:
- *Easter Broomhouse Standing stone* (NT 680 766) Tall stone, cup-marked.
- *Kingside Hill Stone Circle* (NT 626 650) 30 small stones.
- *Loth Stone* (NT 578 741) Single standing stone.

West Lothian Sites:
- *Cairnpapple* (NS 987 717) Bronze Age & Neolithic henge and cairn monument.

Borders Sites:
- *Mutiny Stones Long Cairn* (NT 622 590) Impressive long-cairn.
- *North Muir Cairns* (NT 105 503) Well preserved.

Brochs:
- *Edin's Hall* (NT 772 603) Within a fort.
- *Bow* (NT 461 417) Remains.
- *Torwoodlie* (NT 475 381) Remains overlooking a fort.

Roxburghshire Sites:
Burgh Hill
- Between Allan Water and Dod burn, 6 miles SSW of Hawick (NT 470 062). A 220-yard walk east from the lane. Steep access.
- An ellipse 53'2" SW-NE by 42'10". 13 tiny slabs remain of 25 stones. There is one slab that is 5' in length, however. The site offers fine views.
- *Alignment*: Midsummer sunrise.

- *Condition*: Recognizable.

Additional Sites:
- *Five Stanes Circle* (NT 752 168) Remains of small ring.
- *Nine Stane Rigg* (NY 518 973) Unusual ellipse variant.

Berwickshire Sites:
- *Borrowstone Rigg* (NT 557 523) Ring of 32 small stones.
- *Dirrington Great law Cairns* (NT 698 549) On hilltop.

Dumfriesshire Sites:

Girdle Stanes
- 6 miles NE of Borland, 11 miles NE of Lockerbie. Just west of the B709. (NY 254 961) An easy walk 200 yards down to the River White Esk.
- 26 stones remain of 40-45 on this riverside ring. Change in the river's course has col-

lapsed a large part of the western arc. Stones range from 2'6" to 6' on the north. There appears to be an entrance at the SE framed by 2 of the taller stones, and a kind of portal. 2 fallen stones lie at the head of a ridge 400' to the north and may indicate an avenue leading to the Loupin' Stanes 600 yards to the north.

- *Alignment:* Apparently a Samhain solar alignment to the southern-most sunrise in early November.
- *Condition*: Recognizable.

Loupin' Stanes (Leaping Stones)

- 600 yards north of the Girdle Stanes, 11 miles NE of Lockerbie. (NY 257 966) A wet but easy walk.
- A central circle 37'3" by 34'6" on a platform with 12 low stones and 2 much taller, though mismatched, western stones. To the NW a few remnant stones remain of another possible circle, and likewise about 90' east

of the first site. A disrupted line or avenue of stones leads toward the Girdle Stanes at the south.
- *Condition:* The central circle is in good condition.

Additional sites:

- *Lochmaben Stane* (NY 312 659) Remains of large circle.
- *Mid-Gleniron Cairns* (NX 186 610) 2 chambered tombs.
- *Twelve Apostles Stone Circle* (NX 947 794) Large but disturbed ring.
- *Whitcastles Stone Circle* (NY 224 881) Ruins of large ring.
- *Whiteholm Rigg Stone Circle* (NY 217 827) Low, disrupted ring.
- *Wren's Egg Standing Stones* (NX 361 419) A pair.
- *Ruthwell* (NY 100 682) 18' "preaching" cross from 8th century.

Kirkcudbrightshire:

Cauldside Burn

- 3½ miles ESE of Creetown, 4½ miles W of Gatehouse of Fleet. (NX 529 571) A megalithic mini-tour for the interested walker. Start at the fascinating **Cairnholy Chambered Tombs**, walk 1½ miles to the **Claughreid Circle**, then 1½ miles NE to **Cauldside Burn**.

Glenquickan Circle is 1½ miles WNW.

- The Cauldside Burn Circle has about half its 20 slabs remaining in a ring 82' across. The tallest stones is only 4' high. A cairn rises to the NNW with a ruined cist on top. 2 low standing stones are 75 yards NNW and there is an overgrown ring-cairn beyond them. To the west, across the burn, is a slab carved with a spiral and 3 cup-and-ring marks. ¾ miles ESE is another, more elaborately, carved stone – a schist outcrop – at the NE of Cairnharrow Hill.

Glenquickan
- 2 miles E of Creetown, 6 miles WNW of Gatehouse of Fleet. (NX 509 582) Off the Old Military Road, in a field 300 yards south of the road. Fair access.
- 29 low stones form an ellipse; the tallest stones are in the SSE and are only a few feet high. The circle's interior is cobbled. At its centre rises a heavy pillar 6'2' tall, 3'3" wide, and 2'4" thick. Glenquickan is the area's best example of this centre-stone style. Not far from the circle were 2 ruined circles and a cairn, gone now.
- *Type of Stone*: The centre stone is grey granite.
- *Condition*: Good.

Additional Sites:
- *Claughreid Stone Circle* (NX 517 560) Low ring with centre stone.
- *Drannandow Stone Circle* (NX 401 711) Ruinous ring.

- *Easthill Stone Circle* (NX 919 739) Low ring of 8 stones.
- *High Banks Cup-and-ring Marks* (NX 709 489) Over 350 designs.

Wigtownshire Sites:

Glentirrow

- 2 miles SW of New Luce, 5 miles ENE of Stranraer. (NX 146 625) A 250-yard walk west off the road from New Luce. Easy access.
- A 4-Poster of low stones on a terrace. The tallest stone is at the SE at a mere 2'3" high; the SW stone is lower but heftier. An outlier squats 40' NE of the circle. The area around has many Bronze Age round cairns.
- *Condition*: Good.

Torhouse/Torhousekie

- 3 miles W of Wigtown, 6 miles SSW of Newton Stewart. (NX 383 565) On the B733 from Wigtown to Kirkcowan; roadside access.

- A variant recumbent located on the line between NE Scotland and SW Ireland. 19 gradated stones rise toward the SE, from 1'10" (NW) to 4'4", in a generous oval. The centre of the ellipse has an unusual setting of 3 side-by-side boulders in a SW-NE line. The outer 2 boulders are taller than the one between as with a recumbent grouping. What may be a variant ring-cairn extends NW from the central setting. To the east 415' is a SW gradated 3-stone row aligned NE-SW, on the midwinter sunset. 20 yards east of the circle – part of a drystone wall – is a boulder with a hollow carved in it.
- *Type of Stone*: Local granite.
- *Condition*: Good.

Additional Sites:

- *Balcraig Cup-and-Ring Marked Rocks* (NX 377 443) 2 areas of carvings

- *Drumtroddan* (NX 364 443) 2 standing, 1 fallen stone: nearby cup-marks.
- *Laggangairn* (NX 222 716) 2 stones, Christianised markings.

Lanarkshire Sites:

- *Tinto Hill Cairn* (NS 953 343) Bronze Age round cairn.
- *Cairn Table* (NS 724 242) A pair of cairns on the summit.
- *Normangill Henge Monument* (NS 972 221) cut through by a road.

The Stone of Destiny

One of the most famous yet elusive stones in Scotland is the Stone of Destiny, or Coronation Stone. Unlike the standing stones of Neolithic provenance, the Stone of Destiny is a travelling stone. Stories abound as to its origins, movements, and current whereabouts. Books have been written about it; songs composed; films made; lives changed by it; its existence is unquestioned but its history is a trickster's tale.

The Stone's legendary origins as a sacred object go back to 1700 BCE, to the Biblical Jacob and his special dream about heavenly ladders – which occurred while Jacob's head was pillowed by a stone. It is said that this stone was taken to Spain where it became a chair instead of a pillow: the Seat of Justice used by Gaythelus (or Gethelus), who was a Greek and a contemporary of Moses. Gaythelus had gone to Egypt at the time of the Exodus and married Scota, daughter of the Pharaoh. After the destruction of the Egyptian army during the Red Sea debacle, the pair fled to Spain where Gaythelus founded a kingdom. Then, a descendent of Gaythelus and Scota, Simon Brec, brought the "chair" to Ireland around 500 BCE and was inaugurated on it. It is said that Fergus Mòr, who established the kingdom of Dal Riata, circa 500 CE, brought the stone from Ireland to Scotland, perpetuating the lineage and tradition of Celtic coronations using the stone.

The stone was housed in Argyll (Dal Riata) at a stronghold called Dunstaffnage, until King Kenneth MacAlpin – who in 847 consolidated the Dal Riatans and the Picts into a unified Kingdom of Scotland – moved the stone to Dunkeld, and later Scone, the old Pictish centre of power.

There is a history of profound relationship between Celtic monarchy and stone. In Ireland a certain stone footprint cries out when the rightful king places his foot in the carved print. This print, and the inaugural print at Dunadd (size 8, right foot) are carved into outcroppings of rock – "living stone" – emphasising the Celtic concept of the monarch's marriage, or pact, with the land. Occasionally, as in the case of the Stone of Destiny, moveable rock is used. This ritual inauguration was not accompanied by coronation, indeed crowns played no part in ceremony or rule until much later in Scottish history.

The Stone of Destiny served as the inaugural seat for all Scottish Kings (all MacAlpins, including MacBeth in the 12th century) until 1296 when Edward I, the Hammer of the Scots, retreating with his starving army from an unsatisfactory campaign, plundered some of Scotland's most precious artefacts and archives. Among them Scotland's most holy Christian relic and, allegedly, the Stone of Destiny, as part of his strategy to demoralize, humiliate, and subjugate Scotland. I say "allegedly" regarding the Stone's kidnapping because there is disagreement, *in Scotland,* about whether this actually was the Stone of Destiny or whether the real stone was hidden away and a substitute put in its place.

There was time, and means, for substitution to be made; certainly there was motive. The stone Edward took, and had a coronation chair specially built to house, was of local Perthshire sandstone, about 26"x16"x11"; Edward had iron rings fitted into this stone to facilitate transport. Perthshire sandstone is an unlikely choice for a coronation stone, and of course would be a monkeywrench in the Stone's traditional pedigree of having come from Egypt, Spain, Ireland, or even just Argyll. The Stone's tenure in Ireland and Argyll, at least, are almost certainly historical fact. References to the Stone in Irish and Scottish records invariably describe it as polished and carved, perhaps elaborately, which suggests something like marble, certainly not sandstone; and a rock large enough to be sat upon with regal dignity, which the Perthshire stone is not.

If the stone Edward took is a fake, where then is the true Stone of Destiny? Possibilities leading the speculation pack are: that the abbey monks in charge of the Stone at Scone hid it away;

that it was taken back to Dunstaffnage in Argyll and concealed there; that Robert the Bruce transported it to Melrose Abbey or entrusted it to Angus Og of the Isles who stashed it in his 14th century stronghold at Loch Finlaggan on Islay, from where it later may have been relocated to Skye by his 17th century descendents; that the Knights Templar have it – they say they do - ; that it is hidden in the ruins of MacBeth's 13th century Perthshire castle. The stone has connections with Dal Riatan-linked Saint Columba and the Isle of Iona too; some say it was Columba who originally brought the Stone over from Ireland.

Persuasive stories and tantalising clues support each of these possibilities. But back at the ranch Edward's stolen booty sat in its rack under the chair in Westminster Abbey and every English monarch thereafter was crowned sitting above (but interestingly not *on*) that homely Perthshire rock. Seven hundred eventful years passed. A few tentative, centuries-belated attempts were made to see if the Scots wanted their stone back, but the Scots did not respond. A very eloquent silence.

In 1950 four young Scots – Kay Matheson, Ian Hamilton, Gavin Vernon, and Alan Stuart – boldly, almost farcically in execution, removed the stone from Westminster, breaking it in the process, and smuggled it up to Scotland. For a short time it was left with Glasgow monument-sculptor Bertie Gray, who made at least one replica of it while the stone was in his care. Bertie was known as a practical joker: the stone's convoluted tale was now given an added twist – not only stories about it, but the stone itself was proliferating.

The disappearance of the stone from Westminster created a huge stir. Eventually "a stone" appearing to be the repaired coronation stone was left on the altar at Arbroath Abbey, draped in a Scottish flag, and authorities returned it to Westminster. Though the stone smugglers, especially Kay Matheson, who still lives in Ross-shire and is a strong Nationalist, were closely grilled during the stone's disappearance, none of the four were ever charged with a crime – after all, a court case would have raised the very awkward issue regarding true ownership of the stone.

In 1996 the government abruptly announced that it was returning the stone to Scotland – though reserving the right to take it back whenever a monarch needs crowning. Scottish reaction was mixed. Many were affronted that the stone was only "on loan." Enthusiasm was muted. The return itself was an oddly militaristic ceremony, crowds viewing it almost silently. Was it the true stone? Was it a proper kind of return? The stone was placed in a glass case with the Scottish Royal Honours in Edinburgh Castle.

There seems something strange about the whole thing. Maybe, at this time, the best place for a Scottish Stone of Destiny would be in some cave deep in the Gaidhealtachd, surrounded by the sanctity of the land.

Callanish

I go back through the gate of the mind
Summer being stacked to dry in the long wind
And the stones crouched on the hill.

I'm tired of history as ordered as streets;
The intact exhibits, their questions answered.
I have gone back to these stones.

They are circling in my mind as still as eagles
And in the solstice, a gold chain of eerie light
Flickers in fires on the peat that keeps history
    dark.

The moors of the memories;
Faces that still have their words about them like
    bracken
And the well there green, where the first men
    drank.
Kenneth Steven

Glossary

barrow:
> An earthen burial mound, either circular or rectangular in plan.

boulder-circle:
> A small Bronze Age circle of thick stones placed close together.

Bronze Age:
> The period between 2200 and 800 BCE in Western Europe, characterised by its metalworking and increased social stratification.

cairn:
> A heap of small stones, often covering a burial.

circle-henge:
> A henge containing a stone circle.

cist:
> A small, slab-lined grave, often cap-stoned.

cup-and-ring marking:
> A small circular hollow cut into rock, with a circular groove around it, sometimes cup-marks lack the orbiting ring.

dolmen:
: A tablestone enclosure.

flankers:
: The pillar stones on either side of a recumbent stone.

gallery-grave:
: Neolithic tomb style featuring cairn chambers directly accessed from outside.

henge:
: A ritual enclosure inside a ditch or bank with one or two causeways giving access.

inhumation:
: An unburnt human burial.

kerb:
: Stone on the circumference of a mound.

kerb-circle:
: A little ring of close-set stones.

megalithic:
: Constructed of large stones.

mesolithic:
> Of the prehistoric period preceding the Neolithic, ending around 4250 BCE, and characterised by hunter-gatherer societies.

monolith:
> A single tall standing stone.

neolithic:
> The "New Stone Age" from about 4250 BCE to 2200 BCE when monumental architecture flourished and societies turned to farming and settlement crafts.

outlier:
> A standing stone outside of a henge or stone circle.

passage grave/chambered cairn:
> A Neolithic tomb style found in Scotland, featuring a cairn with a passage leading to an inner chamber used for burial.

recumbent stone:
> A large stone laid on its side between two flankers, typical style in stone circles of Northeast Scotland.

ring cairn:
> A circular cairn, open in its central area, where cremation remains were buried.

1 megalithic rod – 2½ megalithic yards = 6.8 feet

1 m.y. = 2.72 feet

1 m.y. = 0.829 metres

Regional Monument Styles

Aberdeen-shire: Recumbent circles, Late Neolithic-Early Bronze Age.

Angus: Small rings, Perthshire influences.

Argyll: Few circles but many cairns, standing stones, rock art, and line configurations.

Arran: Variety – cairn-circles, concentric circles, 4-Posters, small ellipses.

Banffshire: Influenced by Inverness-shire Clava traditions and Aberdeen-shire recumbents.

Caithness: Large (but few) circles; also horseshoes and rows.

Dumfriesshire: Many large ovals; the major influence is from the south and the Lake District.

Fife: A mix of multi-phase sites.

Inverness-shire: Clava kerbed ring-cairns and chambered tombs.

Kincardine-shire: Recumbents, 4-Posters, ring-cairns influenced by neighbouring Aberdeen-shire and Perthshire.

Kirkcudbrightshire: Central-pillar rings and close-set circle stones; also small ovals of Dunfriesshire influence.

Moray: Influenced by neighbouring recumbents and 4-Posters.

Orkney: Many cairns; large but few circles.

Perthshire: Home of the 4-Poster; some large ovals and variant recumbents.

Roxburghshire: Various ellipses, late built.

Sutherland: Later-built small circles; radially-set stones.

Western Isles: Small ovals with tall stones on Lewis; large rings with smaller stones on North Uist.

Wigtownshire: A mix of central and NE styles.

Stone Circle Shapes

Simple or True Circle – Self explanatory
Flattened Circle –

Type A:
About ¾ of the ring is a circle while
the flattened part is an arc of a much
larger circle, the centrepoint of which lies on the opposite
circumference of the smaller circle. Arcs of smaller
circles mark the "corners".

Type B:
Only half the ring is formed from the
main circle and the flattened
segment and larger "corners" are formed as
before.

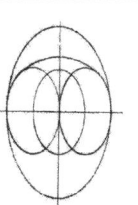

Egg-Shaped –
Type 1:
Lower half is semi-circular, upper half is
two arcs of larger circles joined at the tip
by the arc of a much smaller circle. The
three centrepoints from which the
subsidiary arcs are drawn define two
opposed Pythagorean triangle, the bases of
which are the diameter of the semi-circle.

Type 2:
The two triangles have a common hypotenuse, and the main part of the figure is approximately 2/3 of a true circle, with its centre at one end of the hypotenuse. The tip of the egg is part of a smaller circle with its centre at the other end, and the two arcs are joined by straight lines.

Ellipse –
    Drawn around two fixed foci so that the sum of the difference between each focus and any single point on the circumference is always the same – drawn using a loop of cord around two pegs situated at each focus.

Azimuth

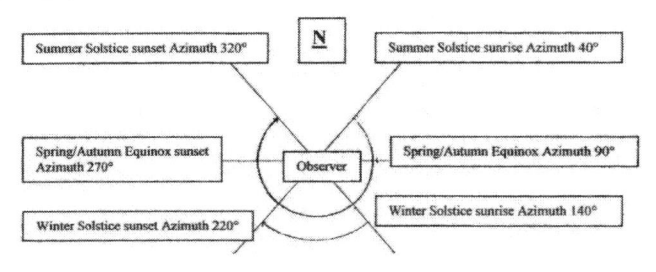

```
Summer Solstice sunset Azimuth 320°     N     Summer Solstice sunrise Azimuth 40°

Spring/Autumn Equinox sunset                  Spring/Autumn Equinox Azimuth 90°
Azimuth 270°                  Observer

Winter Solstice sunset Azimuth 220°           Winter Solstice sunrise Azimuth 140°
```

Azimuth – degrees clockwise from the North (approximate). Variations are caused by the height of the horizon behind which the sun rises or sets. Curved lines indicate the maximum/minimum amount of movement of the sun/moon in a 24 hour period, in relation to the horizon, at the major standstill which occurs every 18.61 years. There occur approximately 13 swings per year. The length of swing varying over the months due to the tilt of the moon's orbit. Standstill refers to the repetition of the pattern over several consecutive months.

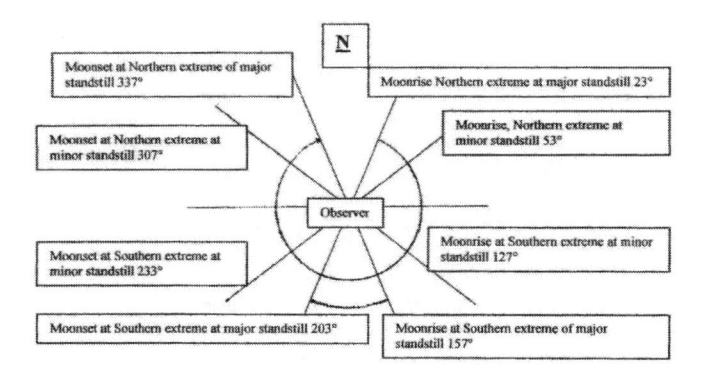

```
                                    N
Moonset at Northern extreme of major      Moonrise Northern extreme at major standstill 23°
standstill 337°
Moonset at Northern extreme at            Moonrise, Northern extreme at
minor standstill 307°                     minor standstill 53°

                          Observer

Moonset at Southern extreme at            Moonrise at Southern extreme at minor
minor standstill 233°                     standstill 127°

Moonset at Southern extreme at major standstill 203°   Moonrise at Southern extreme of major
                                                       standstill 157°
```

Resources

School of Scottish Studies
University of Edinburgh
27 George Square
Edinburgh, Scotland EH8 9
Courses & programs, archives, library, publications

Dalriada Celtic Heritage Trust
Dun na Beatha
2 Brathwic Place
Brodick
Isle of Arran, Scotland KA27 8BN
Quarterly journal of Celtic studies, archives

Self-catering budget accommodation can be found at hostels throughout Scotland.
Independent hostels offer a relaxed atmosphere. For information contact:

> Independent Hostel Guide – UK and Ireland
> The Backpackers Press
> 2 Rockview Cottages
> Matlock Bath
> Derbyshire
> England DE4 3PG
>
> Or

www.hostel-Scotland.co.uk

> Or

SIH Secretary
P.O. Box 7024
Fort William, PH33 6RE
Scotland

For a more structured hostel environment contact:
Scottish Youth Hostels
e-mail info@syna.org.uk
www.syha.org.uk

There are also numerous Bed & Breakfast services located all over Scotland. To get listings of these, or other tourist information, contact:

Highlands of Scotland Tourist Board
Peffery House
Strathpeffer
Ross-shire
Scotland IV14 9HA
Or at web sites: www.highlandfreedom.com;
www.visitscotland.com

Scottish Tourist Board
22 Ravelston Terrace
Edinburgh, Scotland
EH4 3EU
(0131) 332 2433

Bus Services:

Scottish Citylink Coaches
Buchanan Bus Station

Killermont Street
Glasgow, Scotland
G2 3NP
08705 505050
www.citylink.co.uk

Royal Mail PostBuses
7 Strothers Lane
Inverness, Scotland
IV1 IAA
01463 256 200

Caledonia MacBrayne Ferries
www.calmac.co.uk
08705 650000

Scotrail Train Services:

    www.firstgroup.com/scotrail
    08457 484950

Bibliography

Books about Neolithic sites:

Armit, Ian. *Scotland's Hidden History*. Tempus Publishing; Gloucestershire; 1998

Armit, Ian. *The Later Prehistory of the Western Isles of Scotland*. B.A.R.; Oxford; 1992

Ashmore, P.J. *Neolithic and Bronze Age Scotland*. BT Batsford; London; 1996

Aveni, Anthony. *Stairway to the Stars*. Cassell Publishers; London; 1997

Beckensall, Stan. *Rock Carvings of Northern Britain*. Shire Publications; Aylesbury; 1986

Bonsall, Clive, editor. *The Mesolithic Europe*. John Donald; Edinburgh; 1985

Bradley, Richard. *An Archaeology of Natural Places*. Routledge; London; 2000

Bradley, R. *Altering the Earth: The Origins of Monuments in Britain and Continental Europe*. Society of Antiquaries of Scotland, Monograph Series Number 8; Edinburgh; 1995

Brennan, Martin. *The Stars and The Stones*. Thames & Hudson; London; 1983

Brennan, Martin. *The Stones of Time*. Inner Traditions International; Vermont ; 1994

Burl, Aubrey. *A Guide to the Stone Circles of Britain, Ireland, and Brittany*. Yale University Press; New Haven and London; 1995

Callanais. Subsidised by the Scottish Arts Council and Comhairle nan Eilean; Published by An Lanntair; Isle of Lewis; 1996

Donaldson-Blyth, Ian. *Prehistoric Skye*. Thistle Press; Aberdeen; 1995

Dyer, James. *Ancient Britain*. BT Batsford; London; 1997

Feachem, Richard. *A Guide To Prehistoric Scotland*. BT Batsford; London; 1997

Grimble, Ian. *Highland Man*. Highlands and Islands Development Board; Inverness; 1980

Hayes, Andrew. *Archaeology of the British Isles*. BT Batsford; London; 1993

Henshall, A.S. *The Chambered Tombs of Scotland*. 2 Volumes; Edinburgh; 1972

Krupp, E.C. *Skywatchers, Shamans & Kings*. John Wiley & Sons Inc. New York; 1997

Lyle, Emily. *Archaic Cosmos*. Polygon; Edinburgh; 1990

Mackie, Ewan W. *Scotland: An Archaeological Guide*. Faber and Faber; London; 1975

Piggott, Stuart. *The Prehistoric Peoples of Scotland*. Routledge; London; 1962

Ponting, Gerald and Margaret. *New Light on the Stones of Callanish*. G&M Ponting; Isle of Lewis; 1984

Ponting, Gerald. *The Stones Around Callanish; A Guide to the Minor Megalithic Sites of the Callanish Area*. G&M Ponting; Isle of Lewis; 1984

Ritchie, Graham and Anna. *Scotland: Archaeology and Early History*. Edinburgh University Press; Edinburgh; 1999

Ritchie, Anna. *Scotland BC: Historic Buildings and Monuments*. Scottish Development Dept.; Edinburgh; 1988

The Royal Commission on Ancient and Historic Monuments and Constructions of Scotland; Ninth Report With Inventory of Monuments and Constructions in the Outer Hebrides, Skye, and The Small Isles. Edinburgh; 1928

Also the Royal Commission's inventory of the monuments extracted from *Argyll*, Vol. 6: *Kil-*

martin, Prehistoric & Early Historic Monuments; Edinburgh; 1999

Books about the Celts:

Chadwick, Nora & Dillon, Myles. *The Celtic Realms*. Weidenfeld & Nicolson; London; 1967

Cruden, Loren. *Walking the Maze; The Enduring Presence of Celtic Spirit*. Destiny Books; Rochester, Vermont; 1998

Delaney, Frank. *The Celts*. Little Brown; Boston; 1986

Ellis, Peter Beresford. *The Druids*. Wm. B. Eardman's; Grand Rapids, Michigan; 1995

Foster, Sally M. *Picts, Gaels, & Scots*. BT Batsford; London; 1996

Green, Miranda, editor. *The Celtic World*. Routledge; London; 1995

Herm, Gerhard. *The Celts*. St. Martins; New York; 1976

Matthews, Caitlin & John. *Encyclopaedia of Celtic Wisdom*. Element Books; Dorset; 1994

Piggott, Stuart. *The Druids*. Penguin; New York; 1978

Rees, A and B. *Celtic Heritage*. Thames & Hudson; London; 1961

Ross, Anne. *Everyday Life of the Pagan Celts*. BT Batsford; London; 1970

Ross, Anne. *Pagan Celtic Britain*. n.p.; London; 1967

Rutherford, Ward, *The Druids and Their Heritage*. Gordon & Cremonese; London; 1978

Books about Scottish/Highland History:

Devine, Thomas M. *Clanship to Crofters' War; The Social Transformation of the Scottish Highlands*. Manchester University Press; Manchester; 1994

Grant, I.F. *Highland Folk Ways*. Routledge; London; 1961

Grigor, Iain Fraser. *Highland Resistance: The Radical Tradition in the Scottish North*. Mainstream; Edinburgh; 2000

Hunter, James. *On the Other Side of Sorrow: Nature and People in the Scottish Highlands*. Mainstream; Edinburgh; 1995

Hunter, James. *Last of the Free*. Mainstream; Edinburgh; 1999

Lynch, Michael. *Scotland: A New History*. Century; London 1991

MacKenzie, Alexander. *History of the Highland Clearances*. Melvin; London 1986

Mackie, J.D. *A History of Scotland*. Penguin; London; 1964

MacLean, Fitzroy. *A Concise History of Scotland*. Viking; New York; 1970

MacPhail, I.M.M. *The Crofters War*. Acair; Isle of Lewis; 1989

Newton, Michael. *A Handbook of the Scottish Gaelic World*. Four Courts Press; Dublin & Portland; 2000

Prebble, John. *The Highland Clearances*. Penguin; London; 1969

_____. *The Lion of the North*, Penguin; London; 1971

_____. *Culloden*. Penguin; London 1967

_____. *Glencoe*. Penguin; London; 1966

Ritchie, J.N.G. *Brochs of Scotland*. Shire Publications Ltd.; U.K.; 1998

Ross, Anne. *The Folklore of the Scottish Highlands.* Barnes & Noble; New York; 1976

Seaborne, Malcolm, *Celtic Crosses of Britain and Ireland.* Shire Publications Ltd.; U.K.; 1989

Wightman, Andy. *Who Owns Scotland?* Edinburgh; 1997

Site Index

Abercross .... 120, fn. 15
Aberlemno Stone 190
Achany .... 120, fn. 15
Achavanich 123-124
Achnabreck Rock Art 36-39
Achnacree 66
Aikey Brae 174-175
Airlich 204
An Sithean 86-87
Ardblair 177, 199
Ardnacross 73
Arnhill 171
Aucheleffan 29
Auchengallon 30-31
Auchorachan .... 157, fn. 21
Auchquhorthies 185-186
Aviemore 116-117
Backhill Of Drachlaw 170
Balbirnie 206-217
Balcraig 218
Balfarg 207-208

247

Balkemback	190
Ballinaby	66
Ballochroy	66
Ballymeanoch	45-47
Ballymeanoch Henge	47-48
Balnuaran Of Clava	107-112
Balquhain	183-184
Baluachraig	44
Bandirran	207
Barpa Longais	100
Barnhouse	135-136
Berrybrae	173-174
Blackhammer	143
Borroughstone	147
Borrowstone Rigg	212
Borve	88
Borwick	147
Bow	221
Broomend Of Crichie	184
Bruiach	118
Burgh Hill	211-212
Burland	150
Burrian	147

Cairnbaan	39-40
Cairnfauld	189
Cairnholy	215
Cairn Laith	120, fn. 15
Cairn Of Get	128-129
Cairnpapple	210
Cairn Table	219
Cairnwell	189
Caiystane	210
Calanais	91-98
Cape Long	189
Caranais	99
Carn Ban (Arran)	32
Carn Liath	120, fn. 15
Carse Farm North	203
Castle Fraser Circle	180
Cauldside Burn	215
Ceann Hulavaig	96-97
Clachaig	32
Clachan an Diridh	202
Clach na h--Annait	85-86
Clach na Tiompan	204
Clach na Trushal	98

Clach na Tursa 98
Claughreid 215, 216
Clettraval 103
Clickhimin 149
Clumlie 150
Cnoc an Liath-Bhaid .... 120, fn. 15
Cnocan nan Gobhar 84-85
Cnoc Ceann a'Gharraidh 95-96
Cnoc Fillibhir 96
Cnoc Freiceadain 129, 130
Coldoch 205
Corriechrevie 66
Corrimony 106-107
Cothiemuir Wood 178-179
Craighead Badentoy 189
Craighill Mill 204
Creagantairbh 60-61
Croft Morag 195-198
Culburnie 118-119
Culdoich 112-113
Cullerie 164-165
Culswick 150
Cultoon 66

Cuween Hill 141-142
Daviot 113-114
Deer Park Circle 180
Deer Park Standing Stone 22
Delfour 117-118
Dervaig 73-74
Dirrington Great Law 212
Drannandow 217
Druid's Seat 204
Druid Stone 31
Druidtemple 114-115
Drumtroddan 219
Dunaad 41-42
Dunchraigaig 45-46
Dun an Sticar 103
Dun Artreck 89
Dun Beag 89
Dun Borrafiach 89
Dun Carloway 98
Dun Dornaigil .... 120, fn. 15
Dun Fiadgairt 89
Dun Hallin 89
Dun Mor 66

Dun Telve	78
Dun Torcuill	103
Dun Troddan	77-78
Dunfallandy	205
Dupplin	205
Dwarfie Stane	142
Dyce	182-183
East Bennon	32
Easter Aquorthies	165-167
Easter Broomhouse	210
Easter Pitcorthies	209
Easthill	217
Edin's Hall	221
Esslie The Greater	189
Esslie The Lesser	189
Ettrick Bay	66
Ferntower	204
Five Stanes	212
Fortingall	194-195
Fowlis Wester	204
Garrel Wood	186-187
Garrywhin	128-129
Gask	115-116

Giant's Grave 32
Giant's Stones 149
Girdle Stanes 212-213
Glassel 197
Glebe Cairn 56
Glennan 59-60
Glenquickan 215-216
Glentirrow 217
Greenland 204
Grey Cairns Of Camster 124-126
Guidebest 122-123
Gurness 147
Haltadans 149
Hatton Of Ardoyne 176-177
Highbanks 217
Hill Of Airthey 205
Holland 146
Holm Of Papa Westry 145
Hough 66
Innesmill .... 156, fn. 21
Isbister .... 144, fn. 20
Jarlshof 150
Kensaleyre 88

Kildalton 66
Kilmichael Glassary 41
Kilpatrick Cashel 31
Kilphedir .... 120, fn. 15
Kingside Hill 210
Kinloch 204
Kinnell 203
Kintraw 61-63
Kirkton Of Bourtie 175-176
Knowe Of Yarso 143
Laggangairn 219
Lamlash 22
Law's Hill 190
Learable Hill .... 120, fn. 15
Liveras 87-88
Loanhead Of Daviot 160-162
Loch a' Phobuill 102
Loch Buie 70
Lochmaben 214
Loch Of Strome 148
Logie Newton 173
Longman Hill 184
Loth Stone 210

Loudin Wood 184
Loupin' Stanes 213-214
Lundin Farm 192-194
Lundin Links 209
Machrie Burn 31
Machrie Moor 22-29
Machuinn 202-203
Maes Howe 139-141
Marionburgh 158
Marrogh 101
Meigle 190
Memsie 184
Mid-Clyth Stone Rows 127-128
Mid-Gleniron 214
Mid-Howe 144-145
Midmar Kirk 184
Moncreiffe 204
Monzie 199-200
Mousa 149
Murthly 204
Mutiny Stones 211
Na Carraigean Edintian 201
Na Clachan Bhreige 81-84

Na Fir Bhreige...........103
Na Tri Shean............129-130
Nether Largie Mid............55
Nether Largie North............56
Nether Largie Stones............49-50
Nether Largie South............53-55
Newbridge............210
Nine Stanes Rigg............212
Normangill............219
North Burreldales............159
North Muir............211
North Sannox............32
North Strone............1787-179
Old Bourtreebush............189
Old Keig............162-164
Old Rayne............184
Ousdale............130
Parkneuk............198-199
Pobull Fhinn............100-101
Punds Water............148
Quanterness............146
Quoyness............145-146
Raedykes............188-189

Raich 172-173
Ri Cruin.. 56-57
Ring Of Brogar/Brodgar 136-139
Rothiemay... 157-158
Rudh An Dunain 88
Ruthwell...214
Sandy Road West.....................................204
Sannox...32
Scatness...150
Sculptor's Cave .... 157, fn. 21
Shethlin Tarves 184
Shin River .... 120, fn. 15
Skara Brae................................... 138, fn. 19
South Ythsie..175
Steinacleit..98
St. Madoes...204
St. Marnan's Chair...................................159
Stones Of Stenness........................... 134-135
Strichen 184
Stronach Standing Stone...........................21
Stronach Wood..21
Strontoiller 64-65
St. Vigeans...190

Sueno's Stone .... 157, fn. 21
Sunhoney 181-182
Tappoch... 205
Taversoe Tuick...................................... 144
Templestone .... 156, fn. 21
Temple Wood................................... 50-52
Tigh-na-Ruaich 200-201
Tinto Hill... 219
Tirefour 67
Tomb Of The Eagles .... 144, fn. 20
Tomnagorn... 185
Tomnaverie 167-170
Tordarroch.. 116
Torhouse 217-218
Torlin... 32
Torry 210
Torwoodlie... 222
Tullos Hill 185
Tullybeagles... 204
Twelve Apostles................................... 214
Ulbster Stone........................ 130-131 fn. 17
Unival.. 102-103
Unstan 142-143

Upper Lagmore 158-159
Vementry...148
West Cults..185
Westings Hill 147
Whitecastles...214
Whitehill 179-180
Whitehill Wood......................................185
Whiteholm Rigg.....................................214
Wideford Hill................................ 1146-147
Wormy Hillock 185
Wren's Egg...214
Yarrows... 130-131
Yonder Bognie Wardend 171-172

About the Author

In addition to teaching, Loren Cruden has written a number of books: *The Spirit of Place*, which is arranged as an annual cycle of teachings and practices in a context of land-based spirituality. It includes an extensive guide to totemic plants, animals, and minerals. *Coyote's Council Fire: Contemporary Shamans on Race, Gender, and Community*, addresses provocative issues by ten Native, Metis, and Non-Native practitioners, including Cruden. *Compass of the Heart*, which provides medicine wheel teachings and insight on how to integrate spiritual perspectives with everyday life. *Medicine Grove: A Shamanic Herbal*, which provides guidelines for incorporating herbs into spiritual practice, based on direct relationship with plants, and includes a materia medica. *Walking the Maze: The Enduring Presence of Celtic Spirit*, which explores relationship to ancestry, using a journey into Celtic culture and its legacy. This book also delves into issues of kinship, gender, and engagement with place.

All five of these books are available through Destiny Books, an imprint of Inner Traditions, International, Rochester, Vermont.

Eating Diamonds (Whittles Publishing) is composed of essays, poems, and stories about living intimately with nature in Scottish and North American landscapes. This book is complemented with beautiful wildlife drawings and photos. *The Ancient Monuments of Scotland Map (NWP)* is an informative companion map of Scotland's stone circles, cairns, rock art, brochs, and Celtic Crosses.

Available soon through the internet at www.createspace.com will be *Aware Practice*, which is a nondogmatic look at meditation, trance, perception, and lucid dreaming. This book is a distillation of Cruden's most recent workshops and goes to the core of questions about awareness, belief, and spiritual practice.

A number of Cruden's novels will be available through createspace.com also. They range from a fantasy trilogy (*Heart of the Mountain, Coyote at Stonehenge,* and *The Shaman and the Magician*), to magical realism (*The Shapeshifter*), to Scottish historical fiction (*The Selkies Lineage*) and Scottish contemporary fiction (*Local Stone and Debatable Lands*).

For questions about workshops and correspondence courses, contact Loren Cruden at: P.O. Box 218, Orient, WA 99160.

Cheers!

Made in the USA
San Bernardino, CA
17 December 2015